Working Parent Stories

Stories about people committed
to their kids *and* their careers

Edited by
Kathy Calder Haselmaier

Copyright © 2018 by Kathy Calder Haselmaier

All rights reserved. No portion of this book may be reproduced in any manner without the express written permission of the editor with the exception of the use of brief quotations in reviews and topical articles.

With that said, we're eager to support working parents by sharing these stories. Contact us via www.WorkingParentStories.com/contact and we'll try to help you accomplish your goal in a way that is easy, efficient and enjoyable.

ISBN: 978-1-7325901-2-0

Ordering Information
This book is available at discounted prices when purchased in bulk for groups or resale. Special editions or book excerpts can also be created to specification. Contact us for more information via WorkingParentStories.com/contact.

Pleasant Hill Publishing

First Edition (1.1.1)
www.WorkingParentStories.com

Reader Feedback

I can't thank you enough for your … stories. **I really related to your story** *for several reasons … I love my career in healthcare administration and truly believe that it makes me a better Mom.*
-- Susan Sarate, Business Manager

I love that you are including the perspective of fathers, as well as couples. It's very well rounded.
-- Ibinye Osibodu-Onyali, Licensed Marriage & Family Therapist

I enjoy reading these stories so much. I can relate to them and it makes me glad to hear others feel like I do. Thank you so much.
-- JoAnne Nelson, Medical Technologist

A great collective of parenting and career stories from **a diverse group of parents**.
-- Phil, @MillennialDadCo

Your stories of parenting are empowering. And they ring true in many contexts.
-- Working Parent

I really love … what you share. Thanks for providing such a wonderful and much needed platform for working parents!!!!
-- Liz Filippone, Teacher

These stories were written or inspired by parents
who are striving to create strong families,
deliver value via their careers,
and contribute to healthy communities.

Every day.

Table of Contents

Introduction

WORK MAKES US WHOLE	**1**
1 More or Less?	3
2 I Think My Mom Would Have Been Proud	7
IT ISN'T EASY, BUT IT IS WORTHWHILE	**9**
3 Did I Mention the Meltdowns?	11
4 One Day At A Time	15
5 Why Fire Yourself?	17
WHEN OUR WORK HELPS OUR KIDS	**19**
6 Lesson Learned	21
7 Cultural Experience	23
8 Practicing Assertiveness (at age 8)	25
9 The "Best Mom"	27
10 Because I Work	29
FUNNY (usually in hindsight)	**31**
11 Stress Test	33
12 Exact Change	37
13 The Knife Drawer	39
14 Dad to the Rescue	43
15 Laundry. Wait, What?	45
SUPPORTIVE SPOUSES	**47**
16 Couples That Work	49
17 Now Showing: RBG	53
18 Super Spouses	55
ON THE JOB	**57**
19 The Telecommuting Challenge	59
20 Career Pacing	63

BALANCING and PACING — 67
21 Goals — 69
22 Get Real — 73
23 Wednesdays (And Why) — 75
24 Divide and Conquer — 81
25 Sheer Determination — 83
26 It Feels Right — 87

ROLE MODELS & TRAIL BLAZERS — 91
27 Daddy Come Back? — 93
28 Heard, Seen, Validated, Believed — 97
29 Role Models — 101
30 They Say I'll be Glad — 105

TIPS and IDEAS — 109
31 Once-a-Month Lunches — 111
32 Saturday Breakfast — 115
33 Laundry Lineup — 117
34 Is it time to go home? — 119
35 The Dessert Tray — 121
36 Don't Forget Your Lunch — 125
37 More Time (and More Love) — 127
38 How Clean is Your House? — 131
39 From Guilt to Gratitude — 133
40 Avoid Back-to-Schools Bugs — 135

RAISING CAPABLE KIDS — 139
41 Help Yourself — 141
42 Are Your Kids Too Busy? — 143

UNEXPECTED CHALLENGES — 145
43 Charli's Angels — 147
44 You Are a Superhero! — 153
45 The Incredible Challenge — 155

PARENTAL LEAVES and RETURNS — 161
46 My Fear Evaporated — 163
47 Returns and Routines — 165
48 His Big Heart — 169
49 Pushing Parental Leave — 171

50	Back To Work on Monday - NOOO!	175

WORKING PARENTS WITH NEW BABIES   179
51	oh, the places you'll … pump!	181
52	Quick Change Artist	185
53	That time at the UN …	187

BUSINESS TRAVEL and VACATIONS   191
54	Speaking of Business Trips	193
55	When in Rome	195
56	Post Business Trip Reunions	197

HOLIDAY STORIES   199
57	The Pinnacle of Halloween Fun	201
58	Holiday Perspective	205
59	What if … ?	209
60	Christmas Eve All-Nighter	211

ABOUT WORKING PARENT STORIES   213
61	Why Focus on Working Parents?	215
62	Beyond the Benefits	219
63	Top 8 Surprises	225
64	Top 6 Learnings	227
65	Top 11 Insights	229

THOUGHT-PROVOKING   231
66	Employer, Spouse or You?	233
67	Don't Do What I Did	235
68	La Charge Mentale	239
69	Risks and Rewards	245
70	Choices and Consequences	249
71	What Can I Do About It?	255
72	Parents Managing Income	259

More Working Parent Stories   **265**

Introduction

When I started working many years ago, my career goal was simple; show that it was possible for a woman to work full time while raising children. Even back then, it seemed like a modest goal. The thing is, it wasn't easy. Ever. My husband also had a demanding career, so along the way there were challenges, frustrations, and stories that have only became funny in hindsight. But we pulled it off. One day at a time.

While the goal may have sounded trivial, even back then, working parents know that the implementation of it was and is anything but trivial, even today. Some good news is that after our kids left for college I expected to feel the guilt I'd been warned about (because I worked full-time while raising them), but I felt contentment instead.

When we gather with friends, we gain strength and encouragement from the stories we share. Often it is the craziest and most hectic days we recall and laugh about. The daughter who cried for at least five days in a row when we *picked her up* from daycare. The inability to helicopter parent which resulted in my husband exclaiming, "What do you mean you have to memorize the Periodic Table of Elements by tomorrow morning?!" And the annual Halloween costume conversation which started with, "You can be any character hanging in this aisle of the store."

For parents who are working and raising kids right now, I think it's worth clearly stating that what you are doing is hard. And it'll probably be worth it in the end. You're showing your "village" that you value the education, upbringing, and guidance they provided. You're showing your employers that working parents can be strong contributors and leaders. You're showing your kids that hard work is important, it can be fulfilling, it isn't always easy, and you're giving them real opportunities to add value around the house which builds lasting self-esteem. You're showing another generation of young parents what's possible and hopefully helping them understand that both families and careers are worth the effort.

What you are doing matters.

-- Kathy

WORK MAKES US WHOLE

2 stories

The bad news is time flies.
The good news is you're the pilot.

-- Michael Altshuler --

1
More or Less?

Many consider a career to be an essential component of a complete life

Throughout life, we encounter people who encourage us to strive for more, while others (hopefully only a few) think we should strive for less. At least that's how it is for me. My husband comes to mind as a person who pushes me to strive for more, while my high school guidance counselor, who I only met once, surprisingly seemed to suggest that I should strive for less. (When I told her about my college plans, she asked, "Why would you want to do that? It will be really hard.") In hindsight, she did me a great favor because her comments served as a motivator when it did turn out to be really hard, and I struggled. Her words rang in my ears as I steeled myself to prove I could do it.

Why is it that some people want us to strive for less? I'm not sure, and figure that different people probably have different reasons. But at the end of the day, at least in my experience, striving for less rarely leads to contentment. It seems like most people are wired to be most content when they're challenged and contributing as fully as possible.

Which, of course, brings me to work. And the role it plays in our lives. The most content people appear to seek out work (and other opportunities) that align with their capabilities and interests. When people are finished pursuing careers, or during their time off, they're often pursuing activities that look a lot like careers ... without the pay. That doesn't mean that people who aren't employed don't have more free time than those who are. Instead I mean that they often fill a surprising amount of that free time with activities that align with their capabilities and interests.

Forbes recently published an article called "This Is What Success Means Now: Because It's Not Just Paychecks and Promotions". Working parents may find it interesting, and their parents may find it insightful. Stop reading right now if you don't want to know how it ends. The final point seems like a bit of a stretch to me, but claims, "Work is no longer something that you have to do, it's something that you should want to do ... it is the way we become ourselves, not the opposite way around." While that final claim seems to ignore the fact that most people work so that they can support themselves and their families financially, I think they're spot-on in in terms of recognizing that when we find a fulfilling job, it is part of what makes us whole; it helps us become more.

People sometimes asked me why I worked. My husband had a good job; we didn't need the money. The thing was, I wanted more; more contribution, more challenge, more satisfaction, more recognition. More for myself, more for my community, and more for my kids. I wanted the satisfaction and fulfillment that only a career could provide. I wanted to set an example for my children and other people too. I loved challenges and enjoyed the experiences (most days). I wanted more. If you're reading this, you probably want more too.

About the author
Kathy Haselmaier is a mother, wife, and the editor of *Working Parent Stories*. She and her husband worked full-time while raising their children. Kathy worked in high tech marketing and business operations roles after earning a BS degree in Computer Science from Michigan Technological University.

2

I Think My Mom Would Have Been Proud

by Susan Sarate

I love my career in healthcare administration and truly believe that it makes me a better mom

As a wife and mother of two kids, I've always wanted the best for my family. I was raised by a strong mother and great father and feel so thankful that I grew up in a happy home. My mom, who raised me back in the 70s, convinced me that when a mom worked the kids lost out and the mother would eventually be filled with regret. I believed her. Why wouldn't I? She was a great mother and full of fun. She made our lives fun. The thing is, back in 2006, just as my own family was taking shape, she died. She didn't live long enough to answer my questions, understand my family dynamics, or witness the changes that have occurred over the last ten years.

Five years ago I went back to work. We needed health care benefits, and I knew it was the right thing for our family. It was right for our kids, it was right for my husband, and it was right for me. Still, I've been feeling guilty about it. The crazy thing is, the guilt doesn't stem from being "less than" for my kids and husband, it comes from being raised by a stay-at-home mom who wasn't shy about her feelings. I get that her thinking was a product of her generation, but I still felt tremendous pressure to stay home.

Since returning to work, I've come to realize that it really is "right" for me to work. It's made me realize that I was a little bored before. I love my career in healthcare administration and truly believe that it makes me a better Mom.

Ironically, I really think my mom would be so proud of the career I've built, along with my thriving family.

About the author
Susan Sarate is a mother, wife and healthcare administrator. She earned a business degree from Ferris State University.

IT ISN'T EASY, BUT IT IS WORTHWHILE

3 stories

At first they will ask you why you are doing it.
Later they'll ask how you did it.

-- Foundr --

3
Did I Mention the Meltdowns?

They were most frequent when our kids were little

The great thing about a long career is that you can look back, pull out a few nice stories that highlight your "shining moments", and share them with others as an example of your experience. Then you can conveniently forget all of the other "stuff" that happened. There is great value in sharing the good stories to be sure. We all learn from each other, and it's better to leverage the good stuff. With that said, when we only share our positive stories, we may leave others with unrealistic ideas about what it takes to simultaneously manage parenting and a career.

While talking with a young working parent who was questioning her ability to continue pursuing her career recently, I made a casual reference to "my meltdowns". She stopped the conversation. Then she said, "You had meltdowns?" I had to laugh, because all of my close friends know that I had meltdowns, and boy-oh-boy does my husband know that I had meltdowns. They were most frequent when our kids were little, but I have to admit that they started before we had kids, and they didn't end after the kids left home. It's possible I'd have had even more meltdowns if I didn't pursue a career.

By the time I reached my mid-20s, I learned that you don't do anyone any favors when you go on and on about your own shortcomings, so I mostly kept the meltdown stories to myself. But in case others find it at all comforting, let me just say that there were meltdowns. There was whining. There was complaining. And on occasion there was crying. My husband was there and endured it all. It's probably worth mentioning that he also became overwhelmed at times. He handled it differently, but there were times he wasn't sure he could handle it all either. But I had meltdowns more often and better than he did. I definitely "won" meltdowns. (In case you're wondering, we had a string of years when our kids were little when I bet I had a meltdown every quarter. As time went on, I think they may have gone down to a rate of one every five years. It did get better, especially as the kids started taking more and more responsibility for their own activities.)

There was problem solving too. And there were a lot of very long conversations and negotiations that occurred between my husband and me about how we could keep going while keeping it all together. It. Was. Not. Easy.

But we both wanted to make it work, so we did. It wasn't always pretty, but we crossed the finish line. And we're glad we stayed in the race.

P.S. My husband (aka "assistant editor") said that he was disappointed after reading this story. He thought I was going to share a dramatic story about one of my meltdowns, and he thinks other readers may be a bit disappointed with this ending. Sorry about that, but I'm not going there.

About the author
Kathy Haselmaier is a mother, wife, and the editor of *Working Parent Stories*. She and her husband worked full-time while raising their children.

4
One Day At A Time

It sounds quite obvious, but for me that was a revelation

On many Monday mornings (or Tuesdays for that matter :) I used to wake up with my mind spinning: "I am tired. I don't want to go to work. How much longer do I have to go through this? Maybe I should just quit my job."

But despite my inner dialogue, I managed to get up, get dressed, help my kids get dressed, make breakfast, and then, luckily, after the first cup of coffee, I felt better and more energized as I started my day.

One thought that really helps me get through my days now are the words a colleague (also a working mom) once told me: Take it one day at a time.

It sounds quite obvious, but for me that was a revelation. It was a reminder that I do not need to think about how to manage this forever. Just one day at a time.

So now, when I notice that I am feeling overwhelmed by all of the things there are to do and all the places I need to go, repeating that phrase like a mantra helps me.

This is how I have successfully managed to be a working parent for the past nine years. And believe me, I've had some extremely stressful situations during this time. Not only at work, but also in my personal life.

What also helps is thinking about the encouragement one of my mentors has provided. She's told me, "Hang in there. It is worthwhile." And she is right. Once I arrive at work, I feel grateful for my colleagues and the challenges that energize me. Occasionally when I talk with a stay-at-home mom friend, I'm reminded that we all face challenges, regardless of our roles, and I feel confident that I've chosen the best challenges for me and my family.

About the author
She is a mother, wife, and professional at a high-tech company.

5
Why Fire Yourself?

I'd rather have been fired knowing I'd tried my best than to have quit and always wondered if I'd given up too soon

Recently I was talking with a young working parent who was at her wits' end. She has two young children and a high-pressure career. Her employer would be happy if she worked 24 hours a day. She's thinking about resigning because she just doesn't feel like she can keep up with all of the demands. Oh, and did I mention that her work environment is crazy too? The people, the assignments, and the organization structure aren't making things any easier.

I told her that I had been in similar situations in the past and asked myself this question: would I rather quit in defeat or get fired after trying my hardest? For me, it was the latter. I'd rather have been fired knowing I'd tried my best than to have quit and always wondered if I'd given up too soon.

That said, I still needed to find ways to maintain my sanity, so I often defined boundaries for myself at work. For example, I'd tell myself that I would leave the office by a certain time each day, be sure to participate in certain personal activities each day, or limit my hours worked each week. Then I reminded myself that if adhering to any of these boundaries caused me to get fired, I wouldn't beat myself up for it. If I was going to be out of work, it wouldn't be for a lack of trying.

Guess what? I never got fired. In fact, I never (and I mean never) had a manager that even seemed to notice a change in my performance. Sometimes I actually did a better job because I was forcing myself to focus on the most important work and work more efficiently.

If you're at the point where you're not sure you can take it anymore, it might be time to look for a new job. Or you may be able to modify your existing job, on your own terms and without involving your manager, in a way that makes it feel new and more manageable.

Why fire yourself?

About the author
Kathy Haselmaier is a mother, wife, and the editor of *Working Parent Stories*. She and her husband worked full-time while raising their children.

WHEN OUR WORK HELPS OUR KIDS

5 stories

*I thought about quitting,
but then I noticed who was watching.*

6
Lesson Learned

by Ann Brauch

The mistake did not ruin her life

When my daughter Kirsten was a senior in high school, she called me at work one morning toward the end of the school year very upset. She had overslept. And wouldn't you know that it was the morning of her AP Spanish exam. She flat out missed it. I felt horrible knowing that if I'd been a more attentive mother, I could have prevented the situation and the angst that followed. Kirsten was no slacker, and I hated thinking about the consequences she would endure in spite of all of her hard work.

Another mother, a friend who happened to be at school that day, overheard the teacher ball Kirsten out for the transgression in no uncertain terms. Apparently she did not go easy on her. Kirsten was and is a strong young woman, and interestingly, she didn't tell me that part of the story. She accepted full responsibility for her mistake.

Luckily all was not lost, and a make-up exam was offered and taken. I'm sure you won't be shocked to read that Kirsten went on to college, graduated, and is now gainfully employed by a software company in the healthcare field. The mistake did not ruin her life. In fact, I think she learned a lot from it. For starters, I don't think she's overslept since!

As I look back on this experience with the benefit of hindsight, I can see that it was valuable. If I hadn't had my own work and priorities, I might have prevented the situation, and the lesson might not have been learned. At least not then. In some unexpected ways, I think the fact that both my husband and I work has required each of our kids to develop a strong sense of responsibility. And that is serving them well now that they are young adults.

About the author
Ann Brauch is a mother of three, wife, and software R&D program manager. She earned a BS degree in Electrical & Computer Engineering from the University of Colorado Boulder and a MS degree in Electrical Engineering from Stanford University.

7
Cultural Experience

by Jim Haselmaier

Career responsibilities sometimes benefit our kids

My wife and I had careers that involved a lot of interaction with people who live outside the United States. At one point, my wife was leading a team that included five employees in Mexico and one in India. She invited them to come to Colorado, where we live, to do some strategic planning. While they were here, we invited them over for dinner. She turned the evening into a "team building activity" by having everyone prepare dinner as a group featuring foods from Mexico and India. (Since she doesn't cook, and I was busy, I appreciated her creativity in terms of getting food on the table!)

The visitors provided a shopping list and then seemed to enjoy the opportunity to prepare and share the things they eat on a day-to-day basis. (We also collected some new recipes, and my wife and kids learned how to make great guacamole ... while singing "The Guacamole Song".) On one level, this event was "good enough" in terms of fun and a having our work provide a unique experience.

But the bonus benefit was the experience it provided for our kids who were ages 19 and 14 at the time. They were old enough to understand that they were experiencing something special culturally. And the team members themselves were relatively young, so our kids could relate to them. The visitors also did a great job of including our kids in the conversations and activities so that everyone had a great time. It was a special night.

As a parent, this is an experience I look back on very fondly. I'm glad that my kids were there. And it was my wife's career that enabled it to happen.

About the author
Jim Haselmaier is a father and husband who worked full-time in high-tech business strategy & product management positions. He holds a BS degree in Mechanical Engineering from Colorado State University.

8
Practicing Assertiveness
(at age 8)

by "Mom Engineer"

I knew that learning to advocate for herself would be a valuable life skill and knew how to help her develop that skill thanks to my job

While working as a software engineer, I became a mom. I didn't have many (or maybe even any) role models or advisors to help me balance motherhood with my career back then. But, it turned out to be easier than I expected and very rewarding.

Motherhood and engineering are very compatible because each is a perfect break from the other. At work I mostly work on my own, using my brain to develop software all day. At home, I was able to relax while being physical and loving as I spent time with my daughter in the evenings and on the weekends. After spending time with her, I was ready to go back to work and again focus in solitude.

Lessons learned at work helped me become a better mother. One example of this occurred when I was trying to teach my daughter to be a strong and independent advocate for herself. On the job I had experienced assertiveness training and opportunities to practice it. So one day when my eight-year-old daughter's Taco Bell order wasn't filled correctly, and she became upset, rather than resolve the problem for her, I asked her to go back to the counter, explain the situation nicely, and then come back with what she wanted. It worked.

I knew that learning to advocate for herself would be a valuable life skill and knew how to help her develop that skill ... thanks to my job.

About the author
Mom Engineer is a mother, wife and software engineer. She holds a BS degree in Computer Science and a MS degree in Electrical Engineering.

9
The "Best Mom"

by Tina Schmiedel

Insights from an 11-year-old daughter

After our third child was born, my husband and I were discussing whether or not I should stop working to stay home with our kids. My oldest daughter, who was 11-years-old at the time, joined the conversation to inform me that I wouldn't be happy if I didn't work and that working made me the "best mom".

That comment put a smile on my face, because, of course, she was right.

About the author
Tina Schmiedel is a mother, wife, and partner at Sareja LLC where she provides strategic development, engineering, and project leadership consulting services. Tina earned BS degrees in Chemical Engineering and Business Engineering

Administration from Michigan Technological University and an MBA from the University of Wisconsin Oshkosh.

10
Because I Work
by Jessica Duff

Sometimes it takes an outside perspective to recognize the silver lining

As a working parent, few things are as discouraging as not being able to leave work to take your sick child to the doctor!

Recently I ran into this situation while trying to schedule a doctor's appointment for my 8-month-old son for a possible ear infection. As a busy working mom with two kiddos, finding the time to step away to take my son to the doctor seemed impossible. Then a friend helped me realize that I shouldn't complain or feel bad about the situation. She pointed out the silver lining; I am able to provide medical care for my child because I am a working parent. It really doesn't matter who takes him to the doctor.

My husband and I both have busy work schedules, but we make time for our kids whenever possible. Luckily, we have amazing family in town who can help out at a moment's notice. I have a great family, supportive (and insightful) friends, and a baby on the mend.

Who could ask for more?

About the author
Jessica Duff is a mother, wife, and senior account executive at Team SI. She earned BS degrees in Sport Mgmt and Communication, Journalism and Related Programs. Follow her via Twitter @jduff84

FUNNY
(usually in hindsight)

5 stories

Sometimes success is just getting the laundry into the dryer before the mildew sets in.

11
Stress Test

by Jim Haselmaier

I was too stressed out to return to the Stress Management class

When our first child was about six months old and we were in the throes of being new parents, I started feeling weird. I didn't exactly feel sick, it was more like I was feeling really stressed out and anxious. I was pretty worried that there was something seriously wrong, so I went to see a doctor.

Based on the doctor's questions, it became apparent that my "illness" was stress; we had a new baby and my job was intense. The doctor also helped me recognize that my coffee consumption had gone way up. His suggested remedy: cut down on the coffee, try to get more sleep, and take a stress management class.

So a couple of weeks later, I'm in a large conference room at the local hospital attending my first stress management class. As I'm contemplating the info the instructor is sharing, the phone on the wall rings. The instructor stops the class, answers the phone, and the room quiets as everyone listens to her end of the conversation. Then she turns to the class and asks, "Is Jim Haselmaier here?" I raised my hand. She says "Your wife and daughter are in the emergency room downstairs."

Of course, my stress level started to increase even further as I headed to the ER, navigating various mazes and medical personnel. I wasn't exactly panicked, but I knew that anything that brought them to the ER was obviously a significant concern.

I made my way to them, and my wife reported that our daughter was totally inconsolable. This was definitely out of character for a baby who made very little noise and often seemed content all by herself. My wife reported, "There must be something seriously wrong. So I brought her here." The doctor did a thorough exam. The diagnosis: Teething.

By this point I was too stressed out to return to the Stress Management class, so we headed home. Twenty-six years later I'm happy to report that I cut back on coffee and my stress subsided, although I forget exactly when that happened. It's sort of a blur.

About the author
Jim Haselmaier is a father and husband who worked full-time in high-tech business strategy & product management positions. He holds a BS degree in Mechanical Engineering from Colorado State University.

12
Exact Change

It took about three seconds for the ramifications of this to sink in, and I said, "Oh." She replied, "Exactly."

So there was this time that my wife was on an extended business trip. She was out of the country and gone for a full week. During that time my eldest daughter, who was seven or eight years old at the time, was playing at a friend's house. The phone rang, and it was the friend's mom. She was very upset, and clearly trying not to panic.

Apparently my daughter had swallowed a penny and the mom wasn't really sure how serious the situation was. Now, I honestly didn't think this warranted panic. I had vague notions that either my brother or I or one of our friends, when we were young, surely must have swallowed a coin and lived to tell the tale. But I dutifully called the pediatrician's office and eventually spoke with a nurse. She did indeed confirm that swallowing a penny wasn't life threatening and was nothing to be too concerned about. She advised that the coin would eventually pass out of the body in the normal course of events.

"Yep," I said to myself, "just as I thought. All's well." And then the nurse said, "But you have to confirm that the penny does come out." It took about three seconds for the ramifications of this to sink in, and I said, "Oh." She replied, "Exactly."

It helps to try and see the humor in these situations. At least that's what I told myself.

About the author
He is a father and husband who worked full-time while raising his children.

13
The Knife Drawer
by Laurie Steele

Installing a kid-lock on the knife drawer. What could possibly go wrong?

My boys were born when "working mothers" were sort of a new trend. Back then I felt grateful to get six weeks of maternity leave, and there was no concept of paternity leave. My mother-in-law brought me home from the hospital after our first son was born because my husband needed to go back to work the next day. There were no cell phones or Internet communications back then. And ... the thing I am most bitter about: there were no drink holders in strollers.

My husband worked in the field. Literally. He was on an outdoor construction crew and worked from sun-up to sun-down for nine months of the year. So when it was time for me to go back to work, he was leaving home at 6:00 am each morning. That meant that before I went to work, I was on my own in terms of getting the boys ready for and delivered to daycare. Then, after my full day of work, I also had to pick them up. My husband got home between 5:00 and 8:00 pm every night, but there was no way of knowing exactly when he would pull into the driveway on any given evening.

Fast forward to the day when our youngest was a toddler. He came down with a violent 24-hour barfing bug, and I had a serious deadline. I begged my husband to call in sick because I really needed to be at work that day. He acquiesced, and I left him with a barfing, pooping toddler, and a honey-do list that included installing a kid-lock on the knife drawer.

A few hours later, as I was furiously trying to meet the deadline, I got an urgent call (via a landline, of course), hearkening me to pick them both up and take them to the emergency room. It turns out, my hubby had taken the full knife drawer out of the cabinet and set it on the floor. Then, while installing the kid-lock, our sick little baby toddled over, grabbed a huge knife by the handle, and started to back away. My husband instinctively reached out and grabbed the blade, just as the baby pulled back. His palm was sliced, there was blood everywhere, and so, of course, he called the wife at work.

"Are you sure you need stitches? Right now?" I asked. "I am on a deadline!"

He was sure, so I hurried over, picked them both up, tapped the brakes at the hospital, and my husband tucked and rolled into the ER.

I kept the baby for the next couple of hours (until I got the landline call to come pick him up), only to find my poor husband waiting alone on a bus bench with his wrapped hand elevated as he patiently waited to be picked up.

The best part of the story: I met my deadline, the baby got better, and my husband's stitches healed. Meanwhile, I came down with the worst -- and most deserved -- 24-hour stomach flu. Karma. She is for reals.

About the author
Laurie Steele is a mother, wife, and Senior Vice President of Account Management at Burns Marketing.

14
Dad to the Rescue

Stepping in to save the day!

Sometimes as a working parent, you just have to roll with the punches … and try to see the humor in it all. When my oldest daughter was in the 3rd grade, her teacher planned a class bicycle excursion, and our daughter dutifully told us that a certain day was "Bring Your Bike to School Day". This was before organizations used the Internet for communications, and cell phones with those handy calendar reminders were not yet a thing.

On what I thought was the day before "Bike Day", I was dropping my daughter off at school. As I recall, we were running slightly late, so we missed the throng of other cars disgorging school kids. But as my daughter was exiting the car, I saw the mother of one of my daughter's classmates unloading her child's bicycle from their car. With a growing feeling of dread, I asked the mother, "Is today Bike Day? I thought it was tomorrow." "Nope," she said, shaking her head, "it's today." She seemed empathetic as she gave me a rueful smile, knowing I faced a considerable drive back home and then returning again to the school. Also, we both knew I'd be late for work.

But as a parent, you do what you have to do. I certainly wasn't going to let my daughter miss out on the class bike ride. So I told her not to worry and immediately headed back to get the bike so I could drop it off at her school well before the class excursion would begin. And so I did.

Even though things like this can be frustrating and annoying, I remember also feeling a certain amount of self-satisfaction -- "Dad's stepping in here to save the day!" I retrieved the bike and got back to the school as quickly as I could, only to run into the teacher who said to me, "No, Bike Day is tomorrow." Just like my daughter had told me.

This is one of those stories that seems hilarious now. Back then? Not so much.

About the author
He is a father and husband who worked full-time while raising his children.

15
Laundry. Wait, What?

I can't wash them, if you don't throw them down the chute

Sometimes it's the simple stuff that provides satisfaction (and bragging rights).

One year when the kids were little, we reported in our Christmas letter that each member of the family had worn clean underwear every day of the year. It felt like one of our biggest, and maybe most meaningful, accomplishments ;) I used that data point to convince myself that we were one of those really "together" families.

But then my husband, always intent on self-improvement, told me he thought we might want to raise the bar for the next year. As the person in charge of laundry at our house, he thought I ought to commit myself to providing clothes that were not only clean, but dry too. (So maybe his underwear had been a little "damp" some mornings, but it was clean! And that seemed like the most important part to me.)

As working parents, sometimes all we can do is grin and bear it. At least that's what I told him on some of those days when our clothes finished drying while we were on our way to work :)

Epilogue:
Years later, my son joined the junior high track team. During one of his meets he was running in a really strange manner. On the drive home, I asked him about it, and here's what he said, "You told me I should never wear dirty socks, so this was the first time I ever ran without socks." The thing was, I was on top of the laundry! I was sure of it. That night I found about 12 pairs of dirty socks in a pile in the back of his closet. "I can't wash them if you don't throw them down the laundry chute!" I told him. As I said, sometimes all you can do is laugh.

About the author
Kathy Haselmaier is a mother, wife, and the editor of *Working Parent Stories*. She and her husband worked full-time while raising their children.

SUPPORTIVE SPOUSES

3 stories

If you get tired, learn to rest,
not to quit.

16
Couples That Work

Encouragement is how we thrive, develop and grow

About two months after our second child was born, I was interviewing for a new job. I'd spent the previous few years at a start-up that never came close to delivering the compensation I'd walked away from with my previous employer. So when I received a respectable offer to return to that previous employer as a contractor, and in a role I'd filled right out of college nine years earlier, I felt relieved, encouraged, and happy to get my foot back in the door.

But my husband didn't feel the same way. He told me that if I took that job I'd "ruin the family name" because I was overqualified for it and capable of more. He thought I needed to continue my search until I found a position that better aligned with my experience and provided compensation that aligned with that experience.

That wasn't exactly the encouraging response I was expecting, so I paused, and then I took his advice. A month later I landed a much better offer for a position that required the experience I'd acquired and would compensate me accordingly.

My husband's surprising encouragement to walk away from the "lesser" offer really caught me off guard. I'd always appreciated that he supported me, but I'd never realized how much he respected my capabilities. It was a huge confidence booster, and in hindsight, a defining moment that kept my career on track at a time when it could have easily been derailed. (It's also worth mentioning that by pushing me to take on more responsibility at work, demands on his time at home were certainly going to increase, so he didn't have much to gain by pushing me to strive for more.) Of course I ended up taking the better offer, and I never looked back.

It turns out that this kind of "tough love" advice is a trait found within successful dual career couples according to an interesting *Harvard Business Review* podcast called "Couples That Work". Guest Jennifer Petriglieri calls this providing a "secure base" and points out that this kind of encouragement, when one spouse actually pushes the other to move further outside the relationship, is how we thrive, develop and grow. Interestingly, it's often the same kind of encouragement we give to our children to ensure they become capable adults.

About the author

Kathy Haselmaier is a mother, wife, and the editor of *Working Parent Stories*. She and her husband worked full-time while raising their children. Kathy worked in high tech marketing and business operations roles after earning a BS degree in Computer Science from Michigan Tech.

17
Now Showing: RBG

> "I have had the great good fortune to share life with a partner; truly extraordinary for his generation."
> -- Ruth Bader Ginsburg --

According to the movie *RBG*, both Ruth Bader Ginsburg and her husband, Marty, were rocking Working Parent roles back in the 1950s. And this documentary shows that they were doing surprisingly more than that at the same time.

Readers outside the United States may not be familiar with Ruth, who is sometimes referred to as "RBG" (her initials) as an affectionate term of endearment. She is one of nine justices on the US Supreme Court and has developed a fan base recently which includes many millennials.

It wasn't my idea to see this movie; my husband suggested it. But we both enjoyed it a lot. And apparently we're not alone; the reviews are overwhelmingly positive. The movie is informative, educational, funny, sad, frustrating and more.

At one point in the movie Ruth makes the claim that being a parent actually enhanced her ability to succeed by providing an advantage not available to her parentless classmates and colleagues.

Like other stories we share in this book (and on our web site), a case is made within the movie that both Marty and Ruth encouraged and engaged each other in significant ways that helped them as parents and on the job.

I won't share any more, because I don't want to spoil the story or give away the ending. But trust me when I tell you that I think you'll enjoy the show.

About the subjects of this story
Ruth Bader Ginsburg is a mother, widow, and US Supreme Court Justice. **Martin Ginsburg** was a father, husband, and internationally renowned tax attorney.

18
Super Spouses

The vast majority of us need somebody in our court; someone who wants to see us succeed

The movie *RBG* got me thinking about spouses and the important roles they play in our careers. In fact, it caused us to head to YouTube to learn more about Ruth Bader Ginsburg and her husband, Marty, who are portrayed as Working Parent trail blazers.

The search led to a February 2018 interview with Ruth by CNN's Poppy Harlow. Their exchange during the interview introductions, revealed another story about a supportive spouse; Poppy's husband, Sinisa Babcic, who was home watching their four-day-old baby while Poppy conducted the interview with Ruth Bader Ginsburg.

"Behind every great man there stands a woman" is a phrase I often heard growing up. It was meant as a compliment and recognized the value of a supportive spouse; always a wife back then. Many years later I find myself recognizing that there is a lot of truth in that statement; a person or people are often supporting people who achieve anything of value. Maybe some succeed against all odds and without any support, but the vast majority of us need somebody in our court; one or more people who want to see us succeed, encourage us to strive for more, and are willing to make at least small sacrifices to help us achieve "great things". It's the reason we encourage people to establish relationships with mentors, coaches, managers and peers.

We have an advantage when our spouse can act in a supporting role. And when a spouse can act in multiple supporting roles, we have an even bigger advantage. It's hard to find a story that makes this point more clearly than the RBG story, but many of us have stories to tell. That's why we've collected quite a few of them in this book. We hope that they inspire you.

About the author
Kathy Haselmaier is a mother, wife, and the editor of *Working Parent Stories*. She and her husband worked full-time while raising their children.

ON THE JOB

2 stories

No matter how many mistakes you make or how slow your progress, you are still way ahead of everyone who isn't trying.

-- Tony Robbins --

19

The Telecommuting Challenge

by Lisa Giles

Let your family know they are your top priority in the evening. Also let them know that your work will be your primary focus during the day.

Almost 20 years ago, while supporting a family member recovering from a health issue in Omaha, Nebraska, my innovative manager arranged for me to telecommute to my job in New York City. Since then, I've been successfully telecommuting on-and-off for different companies while advancing my career and achieving personal milestones along the way.

During this time, I've navigated career goals, and my husband and I have also welcomed two daughters, who are now 14 and 17. Telecommuting has enabled me to bridge my mother and employee roles, although I have needed to make some adjustments along the way.

At one point I feared that I was focusing too much energy on my career. While I was "home" a lot, I didn't always feel like I was focused on my family quite enough. This fear was confirmed when my then seven-year-old made me a Mother's Day card that showed a picture of the back of my head, as I sat at my desk facing a computer monitor. The caption read: "Company worker". That's when I knew I wanted to make some changes.

I wanted to better balance my work and parent roles so that my daughters saw me as more than a round-the-clock employee in our home. It wasn't easy, and it took some time, but I successfully found ways to find balance between both roles so that I was both a successful mom and a valuable employee and leader.

Telecommuting has been very effective for me and others I've known. I have benefited both personally and professionally from the flexibility it provides, and so have my employers. I learned that it takes discipline to meet both personal and professional commitments. For me, setting clear boundaries has been the key to success.

My advice to telecommuting parents is to let your family know that they are top priority. Also let them know that your work will be your primary focus during the day until they become your primary focus during in the evening. Giving your family your best self, free from thoughts of the work that sits waiting just a few feet away in your home office, is a great gift that produces long-term benefits.

LISA'S BEST PRACTICES FOR TELECOMMUTING

- Start your day early (before your family is awake) so you can prep for the day. There is nothing like coffee and silence to organize your thoughts.

- Communicate the hours that you are "on the clock" to your family. Set boundaries for when you can be interrupted.

- At one point I thought that spending 10-15 minutes in between meetings with my family was "connecting". In reality, I was still thinking about meetings and not truly present in their conversations. I gave up trying to fit in these brief touch-points and instead I gave them my full attention after I had finished my workday.

- A home office can be a blessing and a curse. Yes, it saves time/expense on commuting, and yes, you can work in your PJ's. But it is also your home and you need to set boundaries for yourself. I needed to keep office hours and then leave the office behind. After I clock off, I take the dogs for a walk to shake off thoughts of work so I fully engage with my family. The temptation to go into my home office for an evening check-in exists, so make sure to limit late night visits to the laptop.

- Home office location: my office is at the front of my house, away from the family areas. Having a long hallway separating my work space and my family space gives me time to "change hats" in my commute to the kitchen to be with my family.

About the author
Lisa Giles is a mother, wife, and senior manager of Sales Operations and Compensation programs at Philips Healthcare. She earned an MBA from Bellevue University, and BS degrees in journalism and PR from the University of Nebraska at Omaha.

20
Career Pacing
by Laurie Fontaine

Sometimes we need to take a step back and give ourselves a break

Sheryl Sandberg describes careers as climbing jungle gyms instead of proverbial ladders. I resemble that description. When I set off to start a career at 22, I thought the end game must be that big shiny office with a mahogany desk and some fancy artwork on the walls. Being in Corporate America had to mean we all wanted to become that VP, Senior VP, or hell ... why not the CEO? Right?

At 27 I was told that I had the characteristics to become a VP and was offered my first management role. "Yay for me," I thought. I was on track to get the shiny office someday. It sounded fantastic until "life happened" a few months later. I was a newlywed, building a new home, and found out that I was pregnant. I was beating myself up by spending 12+ hours/day in the office, and I had a one-hour commute each way in addition to that. I was working hard to make sure my team was the top producing team. I had to repeatedly prove myself, especially since all of my peer leaders were men. When I learned I was pregnant, I couldn't imagine taking more than six weeks off after my baby was born. The company and my team needed me. "The team will collapse without me," I thought. Calgon take me away!

And then it happened. This miraculous, perfect human being came into the world and all of my energy turned to him. I spent the next few years trying to be the perfect manager and the perfect mom. I felt like a failure in both roles. Then one day I was offered an individual contributor, work-from-home position at a new company. The new role included a significant pay cut, but I jumped at the chance. My family thought I was crazy. They wondered, "Who would do that?" The answer: ME!

My priorities changed. But instead of beating myself up, I embraced the change and thrived in my new role. It was as if a 300 lb. boulder had been lifted off me. I could now be my best in all of my roles and be present in the moment. I knew in my heart that I could jump back in to a leadership role down the road. And I did just that many years later, on my terms, and when I was ready. Sometimes we just need to take a step back and give ourselves a break!

About the author
Laurie Fontaine is a Senior Director in a Software Sales organization.

BALANCING and PACING

5 stories

To achieve great things, two things are needed:
a plan and not enough time."

-- Leonard Bernstein --

21

Goals

By Jim Zafarana

It was never perfect, nor was I, but we have taken on every twist and turn with trust, humility, earnestness, and a sense of humor

A funny thing happened after I fell in love with my wife, Linda, while we were both attending Michigan State University: 7 kids, 31 years at HP Inc in various global roles, Linda's daycare, volunteering, work at Colorado State University... whew!

We married and then moved away from our families in Michigan to pursue my career at Hewlett-Packard in Colorado. That was back in 1985, so our journey as a couple and as a family has been one of self-reliance from the beginning. It's been an always evolving partnership as our lives unfolded.

Early in our marriage, the stress of it all was a challenge at times. There were deadlines, new jobs, finances, and a young family. It was a challenge to find energy for each other, and I could sense that I wasn't as intuitively grounded as I wanted to be. So I decided I needed to create an explicit framework for myself. I needed to write down not only *what* I wanted to stand for and pursue, but *how* I would hold myself accountable and recognize progress. (Yes, I'm a bit goal-driven.) While this was designed to help me get my personal 'act together', I shared it with Linda during one of our weekly "dates".

See Jim's process for defining guiding principles at the end of this story.

Just the act of writing down this framework and these goals, created a much more intuitive inner focus. And, since we wrote it down as a couple, we discussed it early on, and it helped keep us more "on the same page". I felt more comfortable with our communication. It was never perfect, nor was I, but we have taken on every twist and turn with trust, humility, earnestness, and a sense of humor ... along with an inner 'compass'.

Like that time I was in Singapore on business and called home with a happy and energetic "How are things with you, Bud?"... only to hear that four kids had the stomach flu which included projectile vomiting. And to top it off, they had "lost it" inside the sleeping bags they were resting in. "So, I'm on the way to the Laundromat to clean four gross sleeping bags" my wife told me. By the time I flew home, I had to rush one of the youngest to the ER for IV fluids.

While there is a book full of moments and memories that could be written, I can say that committing to balance and making family your #1 priority can be done while pursuing a kick-butt career! Rock ON!

JIM's PROCESS FOR DEFINING GUIDING PRINCIPLES

Pen and paper in hand, I wrote down a guiding principle for myself:

1. "Pursue Excellence in Everything I Choose to take on." In other words, whatever I chose to engage in, do it to the best of my ability. I also gave myself the grace to not be perfect, and not take on everything.

2. Then I wrote down about six topics I wanted to focus on, and set explicit challenges for myself making sure I could see progress. I needed the personal accountability element and to be sure I was pursuing "balance".

My areas of focus were (and are): Faith, Exercise, Fun, Career, Kids, Linda, Finances

For each focus area, I drew a line from left to right (i.e. bad to great), and listed simple examples of what it would look like to be 'bad', 'good', and "great" for each.

For example:
- "Finances" Bad = Credit card debt > $1,000
- "Finances" Good = No credit card debt & save 5% of my pay
- "Finances" Great = No debt, save >15% of my pay

About the author
Jim Zafarana is retired from a VP/General Manager position at HP Inc. He earned Business, Finance and MBA degrees from Michigan State University.

22
Get Real

by Ibinye Osibodu-Onyali

Sometimes you have to get real before you can achieve your dreams

After becoming a mom for the first time, I had very high expectations for myself and my children. I wanted to be the perfect mom who would raise perfect kids. Parents won't be surprised to learn that my expectations quickly produced anxiety and lots of hair pulling. I needed to get real.

So I sat down and created a vision for myself. I actually wrote it down. It included spending quality time with my family and quality time with myself. It included helping others too. The vision helped me find balance in my life, and I'm happy to report that my vision is being realized.

Recently I was able to show my kids where I grew up in Nigeria and we were also able to show them London on the trip. The vacation was amazing! I had time to rejuvenate, eat tons of food, hang out with friends and family, and I was spoiled by my parents :)

I am determined to help other busy moms achieve fulfillment in their lives via my work as a therapist and life coach. I know that it's possible to be a working mom who has a happy personal life because I'm doing it!

About the author
Ibinye Osibodu-Onyali is a mother, wife, therapist and life coach who helps working moms create balanced lives. You can follow her via Instagram @thehappyworkingmom.

23
Wednesdays
(And Why I Endure Them)

by Cliff R.

I text her instructions so that she doesn't blow it up and burn her hands when she puts it in the microwave

Wednesdays suck.

My wife and I work opposite schedules: I work during the day and she works at night. Four days a week, she leaves for work about 20 minutes after I get home. Sometimes it's hard, but I really can't complain. We've found a way to make it work. It's what we do for our three kids. We have a great house in a great neighborhood and a good life.

Our teen is a cheerleader. Our middle child is in martial arts. Our toddler ... toddles. You could say our hands are full, especially now that school is in session.

On Wednesdays though ... I want to pull my hair out, get Rogaine, grow more hair, and then pull it out again.

The morning usually starts at 6:00 am as my toddler wakes up looking for me. I make him a waffle, and he watches Sesame Street while I get ready for work. At 7:00 am I get my middle kiddo up so she can get dressed before I get my toddler dressed, and then I go downstairs to make lunches for my teen and middle kid, pack myself my own lunch and figure out an "on the go" breakfast for myself. At 7:40 am, we pack up the car, drop the teen at school, and make it to daycare by 8:00 am. That's when I head to work. My wife then comes home from work, takes the middle kiddo to school, and then goes to sleep so she can go back to work again in the evening.

At work, I enjoy being with adults, drinking coffee, and not watching *Toy Story* for the 300th time.

I come home at 5:30 pm only to kiss my wife goodbye as she takes our teen to cheerleading. At 6:00 pm, I pack up in the car with the toddler and middle kiddo and head to martial arts. While middle kiddo learns, the little dude and I go to the supermarket for a few things. (e.g. Daycare ran out of diapers and wipes.) If you have a toddler, you know that "stopping for a few things at the supermarket" is not a quick in and out experience. I'll just leave it at that.

I make it back home by 7:00 pm to figure out dinner only to leave again at 7:10 pm to get the karate kid and come back home. Karate Kid then showers and gets in her pajamas.

Once I finally figure out dinner (THANK YOU, GOD, FOR THE INSTANT POT), I give my toddler a bath and change him into his pajamas. (This, of course, results in the age old debate: monster vs. train PJs).

Dinner is ready by 8:00ish, and we can finally eat, clean up, and be done by 8:30 pm. I make a dinner plate for my teen so she can eat when she comes home from cheer (Thank you, carpool moms) and then text her instructions so that she doesn't blow it up and burn her hands when she puts it in the microwave.

Bedtime is 9:00 pm! Karate kid goes to bed. Toddler and I pick out books, check his diaper, he checks his teddy's butt to make sure teddy didn't poop, and we read a few books before bedtime. He is usually asleep by book three. I put him down and ninja vanish out of his room by 9:35 pm making sure I don't walk on the spots where the floor creaks.

Back downstairs, I clean up the toys, put the dishes away, go check in on my teen that came home during bedtime, and see her for five minutes before she goes to bed.

It's now 10:00 pm, and I'm EXHAUSTED. But I need some me time, so I don't go to bed until midnight. I spend the time watching TV and then need to go back into my toddler's room because he hears me and needs to be comforted back to sleep.

I make it to bed by 12:10 am. And I'm out until 6:00 am when the toddler wakes up, and it starts all over again.

Would I love a vacation on a beach with a cold Corona? SURE! Would I trade all of this for said vacation? Nope.

We do it for our kids. They may not understand now ... but they will. And it's worth it for those little moments like seeing my toddler fall asleep as I read to him at night. It's worth it to see my karate kid get her green belt and kick some butt. It's worth it to see my teen do her back tuck, handspring, spinny ... thing-a-ma-bob, and how excited she is when she lands it.

But I still want that Corona! ;)

About the author
Cliff R. is a dad, husband, and executive assistant.

24
Divide and Conquer

By Kim Darrow

He managed breakfast and packing lunch ... I was in charge of dinner

When it came to getting meals on the table for our family of five, my husband and I divided and conquered. He managed breakfast and packing lunch for the kids until they were old enough to pack their own lunches. I was in charge of dinner. Sometimes I let the kids watch TV while I cooked (I know, bad mom). We may have eaten out and ordered in more than some families too.

To help at breakfast time, after our third child was born, we upgraded to a 4-slice toaster. It was a big help in the mornings, and even today my adult children love their buttered toast!

I went through a phase of batch cooking where I would make a bunch of meals for the freezer on Saturday ... that worked pretty well until I got tired of doing it! I also tried purchasing take-and-bake meals for a while but the kids complained ... they liked my food better! I would generally plan ahead and we would eat the same meal two nights in row. That worked well as long as the meal was tasty!

In general, having dinner around the table was really important to us, and we made it happen one way or another. I miss those days ... even the time I found broccoli in the centerpiece. I guess my son pulled a fast one on us that night!

About the author
Kim Darrow is a Support Project Manager who earned an MBA degree from Colorado State University.

25
Sheer Determination

By Jim Haselmaier

I'm in charge of cooking, grocery shopping and cars

My wife and I both worked full-time while raising our two kids. It never occurred to me that I might give up my career after our kids came along. It seemed like everyone I knew expected me to support my family financially, and I never questioned that expectation. Before our daughter was born, my wife told me that she thought she might be a better mother if she continued working, and I agreed with her. So even when things got hectic and stressful (and trust me they did), it never entered my mind to give up my career.

In hindsight, I think the process of managing careers and kids worked for both of us because we were determined to make it work. Most of the time it was just that simple. We also developed a level of flexibility that enabled us to manage and cope with the unexpected demands presented by our kids and our jobs. We got really good at supporting each other and communicating clearly. It's worth pointing out to younger parents that we weren't great at any of this in the beginning. It took years of trial and error, failures and successes, and a lot of laughter (and a few tears) to work into a rhythm. We were lucky to have friends with similar lifestyles who would listen to our stories and laugh (rather than gasp) and then tell their own similar stories. Even though our kids have been on their own for a while now, we still feel like we're catching up on lost sleep and quiet time.

We each had standing "household assignments"; mine were cooking, grocery shopping and keeping up with the cars. My wife's focus was laundry, paying bills, and "logistics". Over time I added investing and she took on some volunteer work. We recognized that the demands of our careers ebbed and flowed. When one of us was particularly busy at work, the other might need to step in and do more around the house for a while. The fact that we both had demanding full-time careers made us extra sensitive to situations where work was particularly hectic for the other. It caused us to develop a lot of empathy for each other too.

One thing that worked for us was an agreement that we would never commit to a business trip without talking with each other to be sure our trips didn't overlap. That ensured we were always able to honor our commitments. And once my in-laws came to the rescue when we both really did need to travel the same week.

One night, while I was out-of-town and having dinner with colleagues, my cell phone rang. My wife was calling to ask about a logistical issue at home. The call was quick and efficient with none of the standard pleasantries. My dinner colleagues (who knew my wife and our dual-career situation) started quizzing me about how we do it - raise kids while both of us work. I told them that we'd developed a high degree of empathy for each other. For example, I told them that we understand that, when traveling, the person at home has the harder job. I pointed out that I didn't tell her I was out having a nice meal in a nice restaurant and enjoying myself because that would not have helped her as she was dealing with the stress at home.

I appreciated that my career enabled me to travel and change my focus on occasion. I hope it made me a better parent. My wife's career offered the same benefits for her.

Determination, flexibility, and commitment enabled us to make it work. Every day.

About the author
Jim Haselmaier is a father and husband who worked full-time in high-tech business strategy & product management positions. He holds a BS degree in Mechanical Engineering from Colorado State University.

26
It Feels Right
by "The Mama Politic"

Still, it isn't easy

My husband and I both work. I'm an academic researcher. He's a sociologist. We have a daughter who recently turned one and older children from my husband's previous marriage.

For now we're prioritizing my career, although neither of us is slacking on the job. His strong support is enabling me to advance in my dream job as an applied research faculty member at a large university. I feel lucky to have his backing along with somewhat flexible work hours. We also have great daycare which we appreciate. Our caregiver is wonderful, and our daughter appears to be thriving. Lots of things are going really well.

Still, it isn't easy. One of the things I find hardest about being a working parent is balancing career objectives with this feeling that I need to "do it all".

And look fantastic doing it! As the sole cook in our family (long story), I need to get dinner ready each evening. Given my food allergies, this takes some extra effort. And to make things extra challenging, my daughter just started becoming incredibly fussy when we get home at the end of the day. Trying to make dinner and keep her happy is starting to feel like a losing battle. Between my Type A personality that has me wanting to make a great dinner and her unabated screaming, feelings of frustration and uselessness often take over. Hopefully this is a temporary phase.

One way I am staying motivated is by training myself to say, "Screw that!" to a lot of things. I didn't puree my daughter's food when she was younger, I don't make bento boxes, and right now I just feed my daughter everything we eat - spices and all. She has slept in her own crib since day one, and I never breastfed because postpartum depression required me to take a mood stabilizer. Sometimes I feel like I can't possibly be "enough" at home. Interestingly, many things seem to come more naturally to my husband than they do to me. Maybe it's because he has older children and has done this before. Still, I feel like I need to do it all, or at least I want to do it all. These feelings and challenges are helping me learn the value of prioritization.

As I ponder the way we negotiate this life, I think about my need for my husband to support my career goals and understand my need to go to work every day. We are far from perfect, but he definitely has my back professionally. This may be difficult for some couples to understand. Maybe the fact that we both had working moms is why it feels right to us.

Some friends who don't get it give me flak. They warn me that I'll regret not putting our daughter to bed every single night, and they're concerned that I've never cried when I've taken her to daycare. When our daughter was six months old, I changed jobs so I could spend more time with her, but some still seem concerned for me.

My husband and I take this all in. We also know that our daughter is healthy, happy, and developmentally on track. She clearly loves us. Because we need our work to feel fulfilled, we truly believe that we're making choices that are best for her, our marriage, and our family. It just feels right.

About the author
The Mama Politic is an early-thirties mom, wife, research faculty member, and blogger.

ROLE MODELS & TRAIL BLAZERS

4 stories

The work we do, and the examples we set, make a difference.
When we're lucky, we can see that difference.

27
Daddy Come Back?

I learned early on that business travel is exciting

When our kids were little, every single time my husband announced, "I'm going for a run", our son would ask, "Daddy come back?" We thought this was hilarious; mostly because life was really hectic at the time, and while the thought of *not* returning when we left the house had never occurred to us, it did contain a certain level of appeal on some days.

Interestingly, I don't remember either child being upset when we left the house or left them somewhere. They just wanted to understand when we'd be back. Maybe we were lucky. Or maybe they reflected our attitudes that outings like daycare, school, and trips were fun. It was probably a combination of luck and attitudes. And while I wish we could take full credit for the ease with which they handled transitions, I realize in hindsight that both kids seemed innately eager to "get out there" and experience the activities we described to them and they read about in books.

Some working parents describe sad scenes when it comes to business travel and daycare. They tell stories that include tears and angst. It has me wondering if the kids might be reflecting their parents' feelings. It's possible that my own kids may have looked forward to having one of us leave on a business trip since it usually meant a change in routine that could be fun; like pancakes for dinner or a little less attention (and more freedom) as the "single parent" left behind struggled to "survive".

Either way, it may be worth asking yourself if your child's tears and fears stem from your own behavior. I don't remember my own dad traveling for work very often, but when he did, it was exciting for all of us. Not only did he return with stories of faraway places, but he brought gifts; tiny bars of soup and teeny weeny bottles of shampoo. At some point in my childhood I vowed to go to college so that I could get a job that allowed me to travel and collect these prizes for myself. I learned early on that business travel is exciting, and if I worked hard, I'd be able to experience it for myself one day.

About the author
Kathy Haselmaier is a mother, wife, and the editor of *Working Parent Stories*. She and her husband worked full-time while raising their children.

28
Heard, Seen, Validated, Believed

Rosemarie Aquilina sets an example in court

When parents are able to make contributions beyond their own families, they further strengthen their children, families, and communities.

At *Working Parent Stories* we have a single focus; encouraging working parents who are committed to their kids and their careers. Since the beginning of time, most parents have needed to work, but it's a relatively new reality in many parts of the world to have men and women collaborating side-by-side as peers in the workplace. Norms continue to shift as expectations and opportunities for working parents evolve and the value of increased diversity in the workplace continues to reveal itself in new and interesting ways.

When we become parents, we take on the significant responsibility to nurture another human being. And when parents are able to make contributions beyond their own families, they further strengthen their children, families, and communities. This assertion has been exemplified recently via the value delivered by working parent Judge Rosemarie Aquilina. Judge Aquilina, a mother of five children and a grandmother, has presided over the sentencing of convicted criminal Larry Nassar, and she is credited with creating an environment that gave the survivors the space they needed to tell their stories. As CNN anchor Michaela Pereira pointed out, Judge Aquilinia enabled the young women survivors "to go from not being heard and believed to being heard, seen, validated, and believed."

Judge Aquilina is 60 years old. Over the years it's possible, and maybe even probable, that she's had at least a few days when she may have felt like she had taken on too much as she balanced family and professional responsibilities. But the value of her most recent contributions are impossible to ignore. They enable us to clearly recognize that her extra effort has resulted in strengthened survivors, families, and communities. Her work reminds each of us why our own work can be so important.

It's impossible to know where our career paths will lead us, but it's encouraging when we are reminded that when we strive to apply our skills and use them to do the right thing, we are best positioned to make positive contributions. The work we do, and the examples we set, make a difference. Often progress occurs and we don't even realize it. When we're lucky, we can see the differences we make. Either way, the contributions matter.

About Judge Aquilina
Honorable Rosemarie E. Aquilina is a mother, a grandmother, and a judge who was elected to the 30th Circuit Court for Ingham County in Michigan. She earned a JD degree from the Thomas M. Cooley Law School.

29
Role Models
by "The Mama Politic"

I guess it's not surprising that my husband and I went back to work after our baby was born

Both of my parents worked when I was growing up. My husband's parents did too. So I guess it's not surprising that my husband and I went back to work after our baby was born. (And soon; I was back part-time after five weeks and full-time when she was nine weeks old.) I need my work to feel happy and connected to the world. My husband understands and is very supportive. We are far from perfect, but he definitely has my back professionally. This may be difficult for some couples to understand. I get that and wonder if maybe it's because they didn't have role models like ours.

While people don't always encourage working moms, I do think we've come a long way. Things are getting better. Back when I was in third grade, my teacher once commented that she was sad for me. Her comment was prompted by the fact that my dad volunteered to attend a class field trip. Dads didn't do that very often back then. My mom had been very busy with job deadlines, and so my dad, who we didn't see as much during the workweek, was thankful to be able to attend. And even at that young age, I remember thinking the teacher's comment was odd because it didn't make me feel sad. I was glad he could come! When I told my mom how my teacher felt, she told me that people said weird things to her too. She also told me that it was "none of their business". I grew up in Chicagoland, where plenty of moms worked, so it's a little surprising that people weren't more supportive.

My husband also endured some negativity because his mom worked. He grew up in a small farming community in rural Missouri with a population of ~1,000. His mom was very ambitious and ran her own tax business. She was almost 41 years old when he was born, and, get this, he was born in April! That meant she was back at work (finishing tax returns) just days after he was born. He was her fourth kid, so by the time he arrived she knew the routine and just did what needed to be done. Her husband, my husband's dad, always supported her work, but apparently it bothered some other people. While she is considered a pillar of the community, she's also been considered "peculiar" by at least a few. My husband told me that once, when he was in school, he got into a fight with someone who made fun of him because his mom worked. And when he misbehaved at school, teachers told him it was because his mother "neglected him".

Hopefully our kids won't have any stories like these. Lots of parents I know, including my husband and me, work very hard to prove the remaining doubters wrong. And we'd like to think that our parents already have.

About the author
The Mama Politic is an early-thirties mom, wife, research faculty member, and blogger.

30
They Say I'll be Glad
by Chatón Turner

I hope that my example will teach my children what is possible.

I'm a "working mom on a quest for balance in stilettos". My children are seven and three-years-old, and we have another one on the way. I'm a wife to Andre Smith. And I'm also an attorney for a healthcare system, an adjunct professor, and a public speaker. In my "spare time" I maintain a social media presence too. Obviously, I like to write and communicate.

Balancing all of my roles is my biggest challenge. Indeed, Corporate America is still not very accommodating to working parents, and many organizations do not have formal flexible work policies. The culture and lack of flexibility makes balance incredibly hard. Still, I'm driven by high standards and a vision for the lifestyle I want to provide for my kids. My income matters to my family, and my family matters to me, so I try to do it all. I also hope that my example -- trying, working hard, and persevering despite these challenges -- will serve to teach my children what is possible.

One of the keys to our success has been lots of organization, planning, and focus. And understanding that we may drop the ball from time to time. We experimented with outside help too and had full-time nannies that were with us about ten hours/day for a while. Last year we tried going without help, but it only lasted for two months. It clearly wasn't a long-term solution because it would have required our daughter, six-years-old at the time, to give up all of her activities. Right now we have help that includes pick-up and drop-off for our daughter's activities so she can continue with them.

Luckily I have good role models at work, and my mom worked the whole time I was growing up so I know it can be done. Maybe being a working parent is like childbirth. After powering through my own drug-free child birth experience, just like my mom had done, I asked her why she hadn't told me about the pain. It seemed like it might have been worth mentioning! She said "Nobody talks about it because if we did nobody would do it." So, like I said, maybe it's the same for working parents.

People tell me that I need to power through the working parent struggles to get to the glory, and I'm in it for the glory of my kids. Hopefully these people are right!

About the author

Chatón T. Turner is a mother, wife, senior associate counsel at the University of Pittsburgh Medical Center, and adjunct professor at the University of Pittsburgh School of Law. You can follow her via @Chatonsworld on Twitter, @chatonsworld on Instagram, and via her chatonsworld.com web site.

TIPS and IDEAS

10 stories

Success consists of going from failure to failure without loss of enthusiasm.

-- Winston Churchill --

31
Once-a-Month Lunches

by Rick Steffens

I wanted to establish a fun, special and easily repeatable activity that would make it clear to them that our relationship was one of my top priorities.

When my two kids were in grade school, I needed to travel for work a lot. To be sure I stayed connected with them in a meaningful way, I wanted to establish a fun, special, and easily repeatable activity that would make it clear to them that our relationship was one of my top priorities. After some discussion, we decided I would take each of them out for lunch once a month.

When we were just starting out, I didn't really think it was a big deal. But every time I picked one of them from school, the teacher would tell me that they were really excited.

The rules were simple. The child got to pick the restaurant, and they got to decide how long we stayed. I cleared the plan with the teacher in case the conversation ran long. I was amazed by how often they told me they *had* to be back at school by a certain time so they didn't miss a lesson or activity (even when the teacher had told me it was OK for them to skip it). The only other rule was that we would talk about them, what they were doing (in school or elsewhere), and what was on their mind. We weren't to talk about me or what I was doing, unless it was on their mind.

We did learn that eating in the school cafeteria did not work. There were too many distractions and it was dubbed "the worst spot ever". Lesson learned.

My kids are grown and on their own now. As I remember back on these once-a-month outings I realize that what started out as a way to compensate for a concern helped to establish strong relationships and resulted in a collection of fun memories that never would have been made if it weren't for my job and the requirement to travel "a little too much".

About the author
Rick Steffens is a father and husband. He retired as a Vice President at Hewlett-Packard and holds a BS degree in Computer Science from Colorado State

University and an MBA from the University of Denver.

32
Saturday Breakfast

It seems unfair that babies and toddlers don't appreciate the opportunity to sleep in on Saturday mornings

Sleeping in has always been my preference. Alarms can be so harsh. As a new parent, it always seemed unfair that babies and toddlers didn't appreciate the opportunity to sleep in on a Saturday morning.

My husband has always been an early riser, but even he didn't want to get up as early as the kids some Saturday mornings. So early on we concocted a scheme to make these mornings "extra special" for our three-year-old daughter. On Friday nights we'd leave a bowl of cereal and a spoon out on the kitchen table and put a plastic cup filled with milk in the refrigerator with plastic wrap over the top. Because she was getting to be such a "big girl" we'd allow her to make her own breakfast on Saturday mornings.

She was allowed to retrieve the cup of milk from the fridge, remove the plastic wrap, and carefully pour it into the cereal bowl. We told her that only "big girls" were given these opportunities to enjoy this weekly treat. She loved making her own breakfast on Saturdays, and I figure we probably allowed her to watch TV too (if the sound was on very softly).

This scheme provided us with a few more minutes of sleep and helped her start learning that she was already capable of taking some steps to care for herself. It always felt great to wake up fully rested to her beaming smile as she pointed to the empty cereal bowl.

Twenty-five years later, I'm happy to report that she eventually progressed beyond cereal prep and is now a great cook!

About the author
Kathy Haselmaier is a mother, wife, and the editor of *Working Parent Stories*. She and her husband worked full-time while raising their children.

33

Laundry Lineup

by Paul Helbling

It worked. Not necessarily perfectly, but that just meant that there were a lot of learning experiences along the way.

After I was divorced, I had custody of our four children. The youngest was eight years old at the time. It worked. Not necessarily perfectly, but that just meant that there were a lot of learning experiences along the way. As an educator, I think that was a good thing.

One way we made it work was to require each person to take responsibility for their own laundry. As I said, it worked. There were some issues, but I didn't get involved with any of them. When there was yelling, I ignored it. When I needed to do my own laundry and found a load of clothes that had been left in the washer, dryer, or both, I just moved them into a basket.

Years later, when I remarried, I shared this strategy with my new wife who was still raising her youngest (12 years old at the time). She was surprised by the idea, but gave it a try. It worked for her too. Even when she found clean clothes that had been in the washer for two days.

Ann Landers probably said it best, "It is not what you do for your children, but what you have taught them to do for themselves, that will make them successful human beings."

About the author
Paul Helbling is a father, grandfather, husband and retired educator.

34
Is it time to go home?

by Rick Steffens

This process enabled me to show my family that they were important to me

One challenge that confronted me every day at work was determining what time to go home. I get great satisfaction from finishing a task and like to start every morning with a clean slate, but many days, when my meetings were over and it was time to go home, I found myself facing a backlog of action items.

At the same time, I felt a strong pull to get home and spend time with my wife and kids. To figure out where to draw the line and when to go home, I created a process so that I could defend my decisions to my kids, my wife, my boss, and most importantly, myself. Interestingly, in the end I never needed to defend them to anyone but myself.

Here's what I did. At the end of the day, if someone or something was pulling me to stay in the office, I would imagine sitting down with my kids and telling them why I'd needed to work late and miss out on spending time with them. If I felt good about that imaginary conversation, then I stayed and focused on the task. But way more often than not, imagining that conversation just didn't feel right, so I went home.

On the occasions I did decide to work late to take care of something, I felt better about it because I knew that there had been many more times that I'd put work on the back burner to be with my family. This process enabled me to show my family that they were important to me, and to show them that work requires sacrifices sometimes too.

About the author
Rick Steffens is a father, husband, and retired Vice President at Hewlett-Packard. He holds a BS degree in Computer Science from Colorado State University and an MBA from the University of Denver.

35
The Dessert Tray

Sometimes it's best to just play to your strengths

My sisters-in-law are all fantastic cooks. Eating in their homes is always a treat and fun to anticipate.

I, on the other hand, don't really cook at all. It's not that I'm not willing to cook, it's just that when my husband and I were first dating, I made my three best meals for him, and then he said, "How about if I make dinner next time?" That was 33 years ago and ever since then, when I offer to cook, he says, "That's OK, I'll make something." Apparently those first meals I prepared didn't impress him and neither have the others I've made since.

Many years ago we were invited to his parents' home on a Friday evening for dinner when both of his sisters and their families were in town. It was agreed that we'd bring dessert for the group. Things had been especially hectic for my husband at work that week, so I told him I'd take care of the Friday evening dessert. I had every intention of doing that, but things also became busy for me, and somehow the dessert prep was put on the back burner (so to speak). On the day of the dinner, as I finished an all-day meeting at a local hotel, there was barely enough time to jump into the car and race across town to arrive at his parents' home in time for dinner. The reality of having no dessert in hand was impossible to ignore any longer. No dessert for this family of great cooks.

I really had no other option than to purchase something from the hotel restaurant's dessert tray. So I selected "two of each", the hotel put them in a box, and off I went to the dinner with the total dessert failure sitting on the car seat beside me.

The funny thing was, when the box was opened, rather than being ridiculed for not being able to make dessert, everyone acted enthused about the selections from the Marriott dessert tray. Who knows if they were just being polite, but the thing I learned that night is that sometimes, rather than trying to keep up with the sisters, it's best to just play to your strengths and do what you do best. Even if it is just picking desserts from a tray.

About the author

Kathy Haselmaier is a mother, wife, and the editor of *Working Parent Stories*. She and her husband worked full-time while raising their children.

36
Don't Forget Your Lunch

How we eliminated those "I forgot my lunch" calls from the kids

It didn't take long to figure out that an "I forgot my lunch" call from one of the kids created a huge logistical challenge when both parents are working. So we devised a plan.

On the first day of school, in addition to either a sack lunch or lunch money, each of our children was given a sealed envelope containing extra lunch money. They were to put it in their backpack and leave it there all year. (We also told them that this was a secret and that they could not tell anyone the money was in there. We wanted to be sure nobody was tempted to take it.) If they forgot their lunch, they could use the money to purchase lunch that day (instead of issuing an SOS call to us or going hungry).

If the envelope remained unopened in their backpack for the entire year (or was it a half year?) they would be taken to an ice cream store on the last day of school (or around then) to use the money to purchase ice cream.

Interestingly I have only faint memories of how this turned out. I think at least one child got ice cream at least once. Knowing them, they may have called some other parent, teacher or student and taken out a loan. I don't think my kids read these stories, but if they do, I'd be eager to hear what they remember.

The good news is that I don't remember needing to respond to "I forgot my lunch" calls often and my grown children are pretty good at keeping track of their stuff. At least by our standards :)

About the author
Kathy Haselmaier is a mother, wife, and the editor of *Working Parent Stories*. She and her husband worked full-time while raising their children.

37

More Time
(and More Love)

Inspired by Jaclyn Perovich

Thank you for helping me enjoy my children again!

A beautiful photo of a young adult and a small child at the beach caught my eye on Instagram recently, and the caption was, well, captivating.

Posted by "aupairworks", it described a goodbye to an au pair and a thanks to him for taking care of her sons and "loving them like little brothers". Wanting to hear more about this story, I contacted Jaclyn Perovich, the mom of the little boys shown in the picture. She is an au pair consultant so had lots to share. She talked about her positive experiences *as* an au pair and *with* au pairs. The thing that especially caught my attention was when she said she'd told her au pair, "Thank you for letting me enjoy my children again!" His help enabled her to focus more on her children when she was with them, instead of needing to worry about the more mundane things involved with caring for them. Attending "Library Story Time" with her younger son and going out on a lunch "date" with her older son are activities recently added to her calendar. We talked for a bit, and here's some of what I learned about au pairs.

Au pairs focus on your children when you're not with them so that you can focus on your children when you are with them. In addition to keeping your children safe and engaged with life, they clean up their messes too. This means that they do things like feed your kids (and clean up afterward), pick up their rooms and play areas and/or help the kids do it, and keep the kids' bathroom tidy. (They don't regularly make your dinner or do your laundry or clean up after you, but they do give you more time to do those things.)

Jaclyn told me that the value an au pair can provide is different than many traditional daycare offerings. An au pair can give your kids dinner before you get home from work so that the time you spend after walking in the door is focused on them instead of dinner prep. This resonated with me because our daycare provider gave our kids dinner right before we picked them up each day. It was so nice to pick up happy, content kids after a busy day at the office. And the kids were always happy to enjoy another (very small) dinner with us once we'd had time to change our clothes, hear all about their day, and leisurely prepare our own meal.

Au pairs work when you need them; their schedules are very flexible. So if you get stuck in traffic or need to spend a few extra minutes in a meeting, you can remain fully focused on your job knowing that the au pair has your back. Or, in a worst-case scenario, like one Jaclyn described, if you need to rush one child to the emergency room in the middle of the night (in this case it was a high fever), you don't need to scramble to find someone to stay with your other kids. They enable you to focus your energy where it's needed. They can even introduce your children to a second language if that appeals to you.

But you should be warned; there will be tears. Saying good bye to an au pair is never easy. Even when they come back years later for a visit. As Jaclyn told her au pair after one good bye, "Just because you left this house doesn't mean you're leaving this home."

About the subject of this story
Jaclyn Perovich is a former au pair, current host mom, and an au pair consultant who has 10+ years of experience helping working parents find childcare they can trust. She has a degree from

George Mason University and can be reached at +1.571.207.8084.

38
How Clean is Your House?

I need some semblance of order to be able to think

Few people I know find it easy to keep their house clean while raising kids, and we were no different. But I need some semblance of order to be able to think (and I mean that quite literally), so we kept things under control by hiring someone to come in and clean once a week. We actually started doing this the month we were married and didn't cut back to every-other-week help until our youngest left for college.

One of the biggest benefits of cleaning help is that you have to pick up your stuff before they arrive. Otherwise they'll spend too much time just moving things around. So one night a week (the night before cleaning day) we all engaged in a mad dash to put our belongings away. Everyone pitched in, and it always felt like a crisis. There was whining, there were accusations, and at least one of us was usually disgruntled about something. Then, when the task was finished, we rewarded ourselves with ice cream.

I get that not every family is in a position to hire someone to help with cleaning, but every family could modify this idea to meet at least some of their own cleaning needs.

It's also worth noting that the older the kids got, the less they whined about it. By the time they were in junior high or high school, it was just a thing that they did. What I liked most was that it kept things from getting totally out of control, and the ice cream enabled us to end on a good note.

About the author
Kathy Haselmaier is a mother, wife, and the editor of *Working Parent Stories*. She and her husband worked full-time while raising their children.

39
From Guilt to Gratitude
by Shannon Mika

Some friends help us shift our thinking

My husband and I have three boys. The first can legally drink, the second wishes he could, and the third is a decade from it. Not only are the boys spaced across fourteen years, none of us shares the same two biological parents. Our first is a product of my husband's first marriage which ended in divorce. Our second is the product of my first marriage which ended after cancer killed my husband. And our youngest – he was the product of this blended chaos! Like any house, there's always lots going on under our roof. Oh, and not only am I the mom of this tribe and the director of operations for this household, I work full-time too.

Frequently I find myself talking about motherhood with other moms. And guess what? As different as we all are, we're not all that different. Through it all – the joy, the heartbreak, the guilt, the laughs, the tears, the fear, the days we're hanging by a thread – it seems to me that we're all just doing the best we can! I suspect the dads feel the same way.

Even so, I can't help but feel a little (okay, a lot) guilty about what I do or don't do.

But I'm working on that. A while back, a friend posted something profound on Facebook. She said she's trying to frame life with gratitude instead of guilt. Easier said than done, right? Maybe not. The trick is simple, she's started replacing her "I'm sorrys" with "Thank yous." Instead of saying, "I'm sorry I'm late" she says, "Thank you for waiting." Instead of saying "I'm sorry I'm such a mess" she said, "Thank you for accepting me unconditionally."

This switch has really stuck with me.

And once again, it struck me; we all learn from each other. Some friends help us shift our thinking, some accept us on the "messy" days, and some help us understand that we're all just doing the best we can. And most days, that's good enough.

About the author
Shannon Mika is a mother, wife, director of marketing and communications, and a blogger at www.ThisMomShitIsHard.com. She earned a BS degree in psychology from Creighton University.

40

Avoid Back-to-School Bugs

by Jim Haselmaier

It's often possible to stop the spread of a virus within your family

Our daycare provider, who was also a nurse, taught us a lot about how to avoid sharing viruses among family members.

Managing personal and professional obligations is a challenge on a good day. When unexpected complications pop up it gets even harder to keep everything and everyone on track. You probably know what I mean; a meeting that runs late, a call from the school, realizing that you've got two different colored socks on as you prepare to meet with your customer, or a family member that gets sick.

When someone gets sick at home, the challenges can mushroom into even more problems if other family members catch the bug too. And being sick yourself is often the worst because, in addition to feeling lousy, you start to fall behind at work and at home as the ratio of "doers" (aka "parents") to those needing attention (aka "kids") gets out of whack.

We learned how to "contain" these bugs and usually avoided passing them between each other by developing this strict protocol when one of us got sick:

- Always wash your hands before you touch anything in the kitchen, your food, or your face.

- If you're sick, don't go in the kitchen. Period. (My wife rarely cooks. Sometimes when I'm sick, I sit in the other room and give her step-by-step directions. Her food prep skills and patience are somewhat limited, so I keep that in mind :)

- Healthy family members have to become especially helpful since the sick person can't go into the kitchen. Requests for drinks and snacks are met with fast responses and sympathetic smiles.

- Teach children (and yourself) to cough and sneeze into an elbow (preferably their own ;)

- Disinfecting wipes are used liberally to clean off doorknobs, faucet handles, telephones, etc.
- Sick people don't sleep with healthy people

This system works! We often stayed healthy when one of our kids got sick.

About the author

Jim Haselmaier is a father and husband who worked full-time in high-tech business strategy & product management positions. He holds a BS degree in Mechanical Engineering from Colorado State University.

RAISING CAPABLE KIDS

2 stories

Everything is hard before it is easy.

-- Johann Wolfgang von Geothe --

41
Help Yourself
by Mark Haselmaier

This paid off when I was in college

When I was younger, I got hungry after dinner a lot. So I would ask my dad for something to eat. Sometimes he would oblige, but he usually looked at me and said, "Go get a snack. You know how to make a peanut butter sandwich or toast a bagel."

As I think back on those experiences, I remember realizing that I wasn't the only important person or thing in my parents' lives. I learned that they had other things that were important too, and I needed to become capable enough to handle some things on my own.

There was no "ah ha" moment or any great realization, but I slowly became aware that sometimes Mom and Dad shouldn't be disturbed or needed to focus their mental bandwidth on other things. Sometimes I was their highest priority (like dinnertime, when we had something fun planned, or when I was sick). Other times somebody or something else or their work was a higher priority (like when I wanted a snack).

In the end, I learned that if I had the ability to handle something on my own, it was greatly appreciated and generally helped things run more smoothly around our house if I took care of it myself. This paid off when I was in college because I was able to manage most new situations on my own, and my "survival skills" especially came in handy when I moved to Sweden for one semester during college. Now I really like cooking and have progressed way beyond peanut butter sandwiches and toasted bagels. My current specialty is Peanut Butter Chicken Curry.

About the author
Mark Haselmaier is a partner solutions coordinator for Oracle Data Cloud and the son of working parents. He earned a BS degree in Business Marketing from the University of Colorado at Boulder.

42

Are Your Kids Too Busy?

The growing demand for children to get involved in organized activities outside of school is placing unprecedented strains on families

When our kids were in school, we knew a couple who were highly respected parents. Imagine my thrill when I learned that they limited their very smart and very talented son to two (or was it three?) extracurricular activities at a time. While other parents were bragging about the hours they spent shuttling their kids from activity to activity, these parents confidently let people know that they thought some reasonable limits were best for their son.

Their confidence set the example I needed to let go of any concern I had that my own kids might be falling behind because they weren't overbooked and in constant motion. It was really helpful and comforting information during a time that I needed more help and comfort!

If you would appreciate knowing that your kids don't need to be booked 24/7, look no further than an article published by *ScienceDaily* called "Are your children overdoing it? Too many extracurricular activities can do more harm than good." (May 14, 2018) It summarizes results from a small study in England and points out that "a busy organized activity schedule can ... potentially harm children's development and wellbeing." It may provide the info working parents need to better manage their time and protect their sanity.

About the author
Kathy Haselmaier is a mother, wife, and the editor of Working Parent Stories. She and her husband worked full-time while raising their children.

UNEXPECTED CHALLENGES

3 stories

It is the hard days – the days that challenge you to your very core – that will determine who you are.

You will be defined not just by what you achieve, but by how you survive.

-- Sheryl Sandberg --

43
Charli's Angels
by Jim Zafarana

**We had lost our balance,
it was our time to pull together
every fiber of strength and perseverance**

Our journey as parents and professionals can be exhilarating, hilarious, fulfilling, frustrating ... you name it, right? How do we, all of us, "keep it together" while managing the everyday trials and chaos of a growing family? Especially when, for some families, random fate strikes, and we may be faced with a parent's worst fear ... a life-threatening event that impacts one of our precious, dear young children.

A Family Crisis
We were a chaotic, active, happy, motivated young family. Linda and I were taking on life ... and fast! ... six kids, a successful and fulfilling career at HP, a wonderful network of friends and family ... and then, one evening, everything turned on a dime.

Our precious daughter, Charli, was diagnosed with a brain tumor, triggered by a simple eye exam at school. Suddenly we were off to Children's Hospital in Denver, urgently seeking treatment and a path unknown.

Up to this point in our lives together, life's cruel challenges had only landed close to us. We'd lost parents and a few close friends ... but now we faced our biggest challenge as a family.

To make a long story short, Charli endured 23+ surgeries, deriving from a myriad of complications over three years. I used to tell people "we are in a tunnel. It's dark, scary, and I don't know how long it is or when we'll come out.. And we don't know what life will be like when we do come out". Over the course of that three years we were at Children's Hospital (over an hour away) every other month for weeks at a time.

For our daughter, Charli, the suffering seemed unending. When she was between the ages of 13-16, she faced more suffering than I would wish on any young person. We were all scared. There were her battles in Intensive Care and the painful reality of recovery, set-backs, and more surgery. The process kept repeating itself.

We had lost our balance, it was our time to pull together every fiber of strength and perseverance, and advocate for Charli, while continuing to nurture our five other kids (at the time). Linda and I would not leave Charli alone, nor would we leave our kids at home. So we eventually devised plans to cover all of the bases we could; one of us would sleep in the hospital room with Charli at night and then in the morning we'd wake up and drive back home. We passed each other on the highway. Other families provided rides to soccer, school events, and other activities. Of course, we would both be present during a crisis, surgery, etc.

Managing My Career
At first, I did my best to stay plugged in at work. Charli's tumor was not cancerous, so we initially thought this would be a short challenge to endure. But the complications mounted, and it became evident that this was not going to be an easy path.

Enter "Charli's Angels"; my term for the amazing people who reached out with support, love, and human connection from every corner of our lives and from all over the world; my HP family, our relatives, neighbors, and the caretakers at Children's Hospital and beyond. We learned to lean on them and to accept the help we needed. My HP family supported me in every way imaginable. My buddy Jeff took on much of my workload, and my boss/mentor, Chris, supported me genuinely. Everyone lent a hand. Our friend Shelly "quarterbacked" the meal parade that started coming our way. Our kids, themselves affected by the uncertainty and seriousness of Charli's journey, were integral to our healing and managing things. Alexa (Charli's older sister) was a staunch advocate for Charli at school; TJ had to become "man of the house" one Easter morning when Charli was in surgery; and our little Currie was born during the 3rd year of Charli's crisis ... providing hope to us all and especially Charli ... Currie would rest as an infant on Charli's chest while she was on a gurney on her way to surgery. Angels abounded all around us.

We saw, and were surrounded by, the suffering of little ones at Children's Hospital. We never felt "alone" in our suffering, and we realized that, for some families, the battle was even more cruel than ours.

Happy Ending
Today, we are truly thankful and blessed because our entire family is happy, healthy, and stronger for the journey. Charli recovered, and to her credit (as well as her educators and my wife, Linda) she graduated high school and college (with a degree in Social Work from Colorado State University). She is now teaching pre-school in a private school for children with Autism in Denver. Charli is in love, happy, and healthy. As are we all.

While I put my career "on hold" during this time, I was fortunate to be able to re-engage with more commitment than ever. I wanted to "pay it forward" at HP by excelling in my role and by embracing empathy and personal engagement as a leader. I believe in the power of Faith, Hope, and Love, and am forever grateful for my precious family.

About the author
Jim Zafarana is retired from a VP/General Manager position at HP Inc. He holds Business, Finance and MBA degrees from Michigan State University.

44
You Are a Superhero!

**What we do is important.
And most importantly: we are not alone.**

Being a parent is hard sometimes. Being a parent with a job outside the home doesn't make things easier. And being a working parent with a special needs child often feels downright overwhelming.

As a working parent with a special needs child, I recently found myself so exhausted and heartbroken that I was confused. I didn't know whether I was feeling challenged by parenting, my special needs child, or my work environment.

So I did what I usually do when I am confused: research. I turned to Google and searched on "parents struggling with special needs children", and I got a lot of results. There are tons of great blogs and articles from special needs parents, organizations, and medical institutions. It was unbelievable.

One blog entry, from a mother of a special needs child, was especially comforting for me. It said something like this: "If you have come to this blog because you Googled 'struggling with special needs children' you must feel very exhausted. Let me tell you: you are not alone. And believe me, what you do day in and day out is truly exhausting, and it is incredible! You are a Superhero."

That helped me so much. Instantly. I felt validated, understood, and knew I wasn't alone.

Whether we are parents, working parents, or working parents with special needs children, what we do is important. And most importantly: we are not alone in our struggles, fears and feelings. There are others out there who feel the same way we do, and they can offer comfort, encouragement, and even inspiration.

So next time you feel worn out and tired by all of the challenges you face as a working parent, remember: You Are a Superhero!

About the author
She is a mother, wife, and marketing professional.

45
The Incredible Challenge
by Jay Rooney

As she smiles and giggles at me, everything else — my worries, my anxieties, my fears, my insecurities — seems so insignificant

I was newly-married and knee-deep in my career when my wife found out she was pregnant with Josie. Like most expectant parents, we were excited, nervous, and bursting with anticipation to welcome the newest member of our family.

Then, just 24 hours after she was born, Josie was diagnosed with an ultra-rare heart condition called Tetralogy of Fallot with Pulmonary Atresia. (Jimmy Kimmel spoke about his son, who had the same illness, right around the same time.) She was whisked away to the cardiovascular ICU at Stanford University Medical Center, where she had open-heart surgery at just three-days-old. For the next three months, we stood by her side as she recovered. Seeing your child sedated, scarred, and hooked up to so many wires is among the most horrifying sights for a parent. And being immersed in the chaos and isolation of the ICU for such a prolonged time took a huge toll on my wife's and my physical and emotional health, and severely tested our relationship.

But eventually, she did get better, and we were able to take her home (until her next surgery later on). Fortunately, thanks to California's labor laws, we still had jobs to come back to, but Josie's special needs necessitated one of us to stay home and care for her around the clock. My wife, Jenny, having prior medical experience, was a natural fit. Meanwhile, I assumed a breadwinner role and made sure we could keep a roof over our heads.

So now, we went from being textbook DINKs ("Dual Income, No Kids") to being a household of three, with one breadwinner. To make matters worse, a seasonal gig I had done for years fell through, throwing another wrench into our plans.

But as any parent will tell you, we will move earth and sea to make sure our children are safe and happy. And so I did. Even though I already work full-time, teach part-time, and volunteer (along with caring for Josie), I've started freelancing on the weekends so that Josie will always have a warm room to sleep in, so that she will never run out of food or medicine, so that she'll have nice toys, books, and clothes, and so she can build as many happy memories as she can with her parents.

Is it hard? Yes. It's incredibly challenging. I don't sleep much, or well, these days. But when I come home, hold my baby daughter, and look into her eyes as she smiles and giggles at me, everything else — my worries, my anxieties, my fears, my insecurities — seems so insignificant. She is what is important. She's the one I work so hard for, and she deserves it all (and more). I need her as much as she needs me. She makes it all worth it.

If I were to give advice to other working parents, I'd tell them three things.

1. Remember who you work for. Spend as much time with your family as much as possible. Having a child is a gift and a blessing, and we all know how much they refocus our priorities. Make as much time for your children as you can (without skirting your work responsibilities, of course). Cherish every moment you spend together — and carry those moments with you. They will motivate you to do the best you can, as well as sustain you when things get too hectic at the office.

2. Children (and their parents!) are much more resilient than we give them credit for. Josie, an

infant, survived three months in the ICU. So whenever I, an adult, am feeling overwhelmed, I breathe deeply and remember that. There is nothing you and your child can't overcome. Whether it's work stuff, money stuff, marriage stuff, or something else entirely ... whatever it is you're going through, you've got this!

3. Don't follow parenting trends. Parenting fads, like any fad, are fickle — "experts" will suggest one thing now, and the complete opposite thing five years later. But we've been raising kids for the hundreds of thousands of years we've been a species. It's not that complicated; just remember: you're not the first, and you're not the last. Just make sure your child gets lots of love, lots of attention, and learns right from wrong. Everything else, you'll figure out. (However, DO seek out groups of parents to talk and listen to, and seek support from those who've been there before. Especially if your child struggles with illness or has other special needs)

Parenting is life's most challenging endeavor. But it's also the most rewarding. My love for Josie knows no bounds, and anytime she falls asleep in my arms, I know that no matter how tough things get, and no matter how many problems I'm facing, everything is fine, and everything will be fine.

If you can relate to that last paragraph, don't worry — chances are, you're doing it right!

About the author

Jay Rooney is a Freelance Commercial Writer, University Professor, Self-Published Author, and Publicist who holds a MS in Integrated Marketing Communications from Golden Gate University. He offers copywriting, copyediting, and brand storytelling solutions to small businesses, nonprofits, and marketing agencies in the San Francisco Bay Area and nationwide. Keep up with his (and Josie's) journey by following @RamblingRooney on Twitter.

PARENTAL LEAVES and RETURNING TO WORK

5 stories

If I quit now, I will soon be back to where I started.

And when I started, I was desperately wishing to be where I am now.

46
My Fear Evaporated

by Kelsey Sprowell

Returning to work after parental leave

I had a lot of fear about going back to work after my daughter was born. My own mom, whom I admire, didn't work after I was born.

That fear completely evaporated after about six months! My initial fear was probably common; I just couldn't imagine that anyone else could possibly love my daughter and take care of her the way I do. But I noticed right away that she came home from "school" smelling like her teachers, so I knew she was being held all day, and that was reassuring. Also, she never cried when I dropped her off, which helped. And every time we got to school, all of the teachers addressed her (not me) - "Hi Olivia!"

I was also nervous about missing out. I didn't want to miss her first steps, for instance. But what I've found is that the work week is really short, and I don't miss much. I don't ever get annoyed or fed up with her because we're just not together long enough to get on each other's nerves.

I love my job, and the people I work with, so before Olivia was born (and after), I couldn't imagine staying home. I get so much fulfillment from working and being a mom.

About the author
Kelsey Sprowell is a mother, wife, and strategic relationship manager at Zen Planner. She holds a BS degree in Biochemistry from Colorado State University and an MS degree in Systematic & Philosophical Theology from Pacific Lutheran Theological Seminary.

47
Returns and Routines

**Most kids need routine.
Be sure to establish them before heading back to work after an extended leave.**

If you're planning to re-enter the workforce after an extended break, and you have kids that aren't newborns, it might help to consider the change from their point of view. Most kids find comfort in routine, so at least starting to establish a new routine, before you actually start the job, is likely to make the transition easier on everyone.

Think ahead. Chances are that you will need your kids to do more for themselves if you're going back to work. Asking them to take on more responsibilities around the house is great for them, and it should help you too.

The key to a smooth transition is to be sure that your kids have taken on these new responsibilities before your first day on the job. Even relatively compliant kids will need "practice" before new routines run smoothly. We found that our kids usually threw three "fits" in a row when we imposed new routines on them. If we could endure those "fits" (which usually were just complaints, whines or worse), and stay firm (and consistent), the new routine tended to click by the fourth iteration and the kids often became enthusiasts. Maybe we're all that way :)

Here are ideas for things most kids can be expected to take on around the house. Obviously their ability to take on various responsibilities will vary widely based on their ages.

- Dress themselves (Layout their clothes the night before. Or, some parents admit that they put their toddlers to bed in the next day's outfit.)
- Get their own breakfast
- Pack a school lunch
- Help with dinner
- Get their own snacks
- Vacuum, dust and/or prep for cleaning help (you may need it!)
- Feed, walk, and/or clean up after the pet(s)
- Do their own laundry
- Take out the trash
- Help in the yard
- Let you sleep in on the weekends!

Most kids are happy to help when they know that their contributions are meaningful; it gives them a great sense of accomplishment and helps build lasting self-esteem. This means that while they're taking on a new responsibility you need to be sure you're not hovering over them, offering too many suggestions, and/or criticizing their efforts. Let them make a few mistakes! Keep yourself busy doing something else meaningful while they tackle their new "jobs".

An important key to success is to be sure that your kids don't view your return to work as an imposition on their routines or a punishment. By establishing new routines before your return, you're likely to ease the transition for everyone and discover how your work actually helps your kids become more capable adults in the future.

Good luck!

About the author
Kathy Haselmaier is a mother, wife, and the editor of Working Parent Stories. She and her husband worked full-time while raising their children.

48
His Big Heart
by "Mom2Boys"

It made my mom heart want to burst

I am not the mom who cries when dropping her kids off, but as I prepared to return to work after completing my parental leave it was a little different. Our baby was attending his first day at school with his "experienced" big brother.

I can't begin to tell you how much we absolutely love our kids' teachers, which is why I was positive I wouldn't cry when I put them in such good hands. I was doing well, dry eyes and everything, until I turned to walk out of the infant room and saw my older son's concern for his little brother; he was peering through a window checking on his baby brother as I left the room. His big heart was so obvious, and I could see him caring about and being protective of his little brother. It made my mom heart want to burst, but instead my eyes welled with tears.

Later their teachers let me know that my older son insisted on visiting his baby brother multiple times throughout the day just to make sure he was adjusting well. I can't imagine loving these boys any more and appreciate their caring teachers so much!

About the author
Mom2Boys is a mother, wife, and global product manager at a high-tech company. She earned an MBA degree at university in the United States.

49
Pushing Parental Leave

by Jim Haselmaier

If you want to be a change agent, you sometimes need to be willing to take at least a small hit

My wife and I worked full-time while we raised our kids. We were at the same big company during most of those years, so in retrospect, our somewhat common work environment provided an interesting view into how one company treated working parents. We compared notes in a variety of situations, and by and large, we both felt like we were treated well and fairly. And we hoped, in some small way, we paved the way for other parents wanting to follow a similar path.

When our first child was born there was no FMLA (Family and Medical Leave Act) in the US. If an employee working for our company gave birth, she was offered a benefit that provided six weeks of partially paid medical leave, with an option to take up to two additional months of unpaid maternity leave. As we planned for our baby, we planned for the unpaid time off. The benefit stipulated that upon her return to work, the new mother was guaranteed a job at the same level she'd had before taking the leave. It was a sweet deal, and we appreciated it.

While this benefit was attractive to us, my wife and I both wanted to spend time with our newborn. And while we appreciated the maternity benefits offered, my options were a lot more limited and my status was not as well protected. We decided that rather than take a lot of time off together, I'd take the majority of my time off when my wife returned to work. We thought that four weeks at home for me would work well.

We worked with the company to arrange a plan that made sense to us, but we were confused as we tried to understand why the company thought mothers should take time off with babies, but not fathers. As we were investigating how to make this happen, I vividly remember us sitting in the office of an HR manager discussing the situation. He very clearly told me: "You can take vacation time. And we might be able to find a way for you to take unpaid time off." My response was immediate and clear: "When my wife finishes her medical leave there is no difference between us. Why does she get a maternity leave and I do not get a paternity leave?" HR's response was, "That's the way it is." In an attempt to help us achieve our goal, the HR manager suggested that I could claim the time off would be spent caring for my father, who was ill at the time, but I had no interest in twisting the truth.

We pushed forward to make it happen, but conversations with my manager didn't go any better. He told me that if I took the four weeks off, he'd have a job for me when I returned, but I would be demoted from my management position, so I'd return at a lower level. That only strengthened our resolve to make it happen. In the end, I stayed home for four weeks after my wife returned to work.

The time at home alone with my baby daughter was fantastic. I mastered every aspect of her care, and we went on outings together. It was great to have that dedicated time with the newest member of our family.

Interestingly, things at work went better than expected in the end. During the middle of my leave, my manager called me and said, "We had a manager leave. When you return, would you be willing to return as a manager?" I told him, "Well, as a matter of fact, I would!"

In hindsight, this was one of the best outcomes I've experienced after being forced to make what seemed like a difficult decision (at the time). Twenty-seven years later I'm not missing the four weeks of 1990 pay, I don't think it hurt my career, and I'd like to think that I may have helped plant a few ideas in the minds of HR and management that have supported new benefits that exist today.

It's easy to complain about things not being the way you want them to be, but if you want to be a change agent, you sometimes need to be willing to take at least a small hit so that things will be better for others in the future. We're glad that our small step back in 1990 may have helped change things just a little and hope you might consider doing something similar if an opportunity presents itself to you.

About the author
Jim Haselmaier is a father and husband who worked full-time in high-tech business strategy & product management positions. He holds a BS degree in Mechanical Engineering from Colorado State University.

50

I Have To Go Back To Work on Monday - NOOOOOO!

by Andrew P.

The bacon must be brought, the bread must be won

I turned 30 when my wife was six months pregnant, and now our son is just over a month old. I am lucky enough to work for a company that provides four weeks of paid leave for fathers, but that's just about over, and the thought of being back at work has me grunting with disgust.

I'm a rather excellent employee - if I do say so myself. But hell, I'm a millennial and the most important thing in my life is the stretch of hours from 5pm-8am and any vacation time I can swindle with my family in our fairly modest, yet perfect, 1,500 square feet of home. Work is my priority when I'm there, sure, but you're never going to see me staying in the office past 5:00 pm unless I have to. That's what laptops are for. I don't mind working from home, as long as I'm home.

I felt that way *before* we had a child, and now that we have a perfect little human with all of his faces and noises and adorable bodily functions, that feeling has grown exponentially. How am I going to spend nine hours a day away from all this wonder that I've built? If I had the choice, I would stay home with my wife and son and write fiction for a couple hours a day ... and that's it.

But we don't have that choice, do we? The bacon must be brought, the bread must be won.

I hold a fairly low-level marketing position at my company, and while I know I am privileged by the job and salary, I know (because math) that I don't make enough to cover the mortgage and expenses in full without dipping into savings a little every month and accepting a little credit card debt chaser: the delicate balance of capitalism. So I have some rapid growth to do and I need to do it yesterday.

It's pressure and expectation and anxiety that I really don't want. What I want is to revel in my new life as a father, but that just isn't a possibility. All of this reality has come crashing back at me in larger and larger waves every day for the last week as

Monday looms. *Working Parent Stories* wanted me to talk about how I'm feeling as I wrap up my parental leave, and the short answer is this: dismally.

Alright, but I'm really not that defeatist. I may sigh and complain, but actually, I'm as strong as hell and I'm going to push, and I'm going to grow, and I'm going to be home at 5:20 p.m. to give my son more kisses than he can handle.

About the author
Andrew P. is a father, husband, and marketing professional living in Vermont.

WORKING PARENTS WITH NEW BABIES

3 stories

Instead of thinking how hard your journey is,
think how great your story will be.

-- Andy Frisella --

51
oh, the places you'll … pump!

by "Human Rights Mama"

It's often hard to find places to pump or nurse when you're away from home; especially in big cities

As a lawyer specializing in policy advocacy for refugee rights and the mother of two, I've found myself pumping in a wide variety of places including New York City, Geneva, Washington, DC, Las Vegas, and Brussels. (Not to mention on airplanes to said destinations.) I have also purchased pump replacement parts in nearly all of these cities as I seem to forget one key part on every single trip. Target stores are a blessing to all women who need quick pumping solutions!

Figuring out where to pump can be a challenge. On many trips I need to walk or take transit between multiple meetings in a single day. It's often hard to find places to pump or nurse when I'm away from home and on the go; especially in big cities. Thankfully there are some apps and websites that crowdsource good places to pump, including momspumphere.com. When in doubt, I've found it helps to ask the Internet.

Hotels have been the most accommodating in my experience. They usually offer me an empty room or an office, even if I'm not a guest. And like many, I've had to settle for the gross public restroom on occasion.

Airports often have lactation or baby rooms now, which is incredibly helpful. San Francisco International Airport has a great room on the new pier in Terminal 3; it has become one of my favorite stops before boarding a plane.

My favorite ad hoc location was a Nordstrom dressing room near Washington, DC. It was quite comfortable, though I am sure the other patrons were a bit confused by the mechanical sounds coming from my room :)

And what to do with all that milk? Thankfully there are services available to ship it home in a chilled container. I've used Milk Stork, and FedEx has options as well.

About the author
Human Rights Mama is a mother, wife and lawyer specializing in refugee rights policy advocacy. At work she leads a team that leverages volunteer lawyers to help meet the legal needs of Californians.

52
Quick Change Artist
by "Human Rights Mama"

I put the baby down for a nap and pulled a blazer on over a nursing shirt

Remember the video of the man who was being interviewed by the BBC live when his toddler walked into the room? That is probably every work-from-home parent's nightmare, and I was thinking about it recently when I was asked to create a "welcome video" to introduce myself as a tutor for an online course on refugee protection.

Online learning and virtual workplaces are magical inventions for working parents with small children. No one needs to know that you are in your pajamas, or haven't showered for a couple of days, as long as your brain is clear and your fingers type swiftly. Unless, of course, you need to be on video.

As the mother of a 10-week-old, I don't currently go into an office during the day, and I don't have the luxury of time. While my baby isn't mobile, her little voice travels in my small apartment, so I'm pretty proud of the fact that I was able to create and post a video recently. And it was done on time, and I looked (at least theoretically) polished. The technique? I put on some makeup very early in the morning. Later that day, I put the baby down for a nap, pulled a blazer on over a nursing shirt, clipped my hair back, found a good backdrop (a bookshelf), and filmed the whole thing before she even woke up.

As Leonard Bernstein once said, "To achieve success, two things are needed; a plan and not enough time." I concur.

About the author
Human Rights Mama is a mother, wife and lawyer specializing in refugee rights policy advocacy. At work she leads a team that leverages volunteer lawyers to help meet the legal needs of Californians.

53
That time at the UN …

by "Human Rights Mama"

I've had a number of experiences that only seem 'funny' in hindsight

As a lawyer and the mother of a three-year-old and ten-week-old, I've had a number of experiences that only seem "funny" in hindsight. I share them in an effort to encourage other working parents because it isn't always easy, but we get the job done (at work and at home)!

When my son, our first child, was three and a half months old, I took a required work trip to a conference in Europe. It was my second week back from maternity leave and my employer was very supportive, encouraging me to bring my spouse and baby along. Having them close enabled me to more easily focus on my work; leading a staff retreat and attending human rights hearings at the United Nations all week. My husband was extremely supportive and happy to come along to help, but the universe kept throwing obstacles in our way. At the time I was exclusively breastfeeding and quickly discovered that I did not have the right electrical adapters to enable me to pump. Plus there weren't many electrical outlets in the city restrooms anyway.

As if that wasn't enough of a challenge, it was 100°F outside, and it was humid too. But we made it work.

Instead of seeing some sights as he'd planned, my husband brought the baby to me every three hours for feedings. The thing was, my husband rarely had the right badges to get into the buildings, so he had to wait for me out in the heat. Or sometimes we met in an air-conditioned grocery store to pass the baby back and forth. Then he would pack our little boy up and try to get him somewhere cool for a nap. He must have logged 50 miles of walking that week!

In one of my favorite moments, the UN refused to let the baby through security because he didn't have an official badge from an accredited organization. That meant that I missed an entire afternoon of hearings at the Human Rights Council. I believe they were talking about women's rights in that session …

The irony was not lost on me.

About the author

Human Rights Mama is a mother, wife and lawyer specializing in human and refugee rights advocacy and nonprofit leadership. At work she leads a team that leverages volunteer lawyers to help meet the legal needs of all Californians.

BUSINESS TRAVEL and VACATIONS

3 stories

There are no traffic jams along the extra mile.

-- Roger Staubach --

54

Speaking of Business Trips

Inspired by Anne McClain

Gotta play the long game here

Some working parents fret about the need to travel for business. Astronaut Anne McClain, who will be heading to the International Space Station in November (2018), offers a balanced perspective shared by many. Some of her thoughts have been included in a short *Yahoo! Lifestyle* video. When asked if it's more difficult to stay back from expeditions or to leave for them, McClain replied: "No easy answer there. One provides immediate comfort, the other achieves not only lifelong goals but also teaches lifelong lessons. Gotta play the long game here … most parents can relate."

Anne will be away from home for six months. How long will you be gone?
About the subject of this story

Anne McClain is a mother, wife, NASA astronaut, and Major in the U.S. Army.

55
When in Rome

Work experiences often make us better parents

Work required me to travel internationally on occasion. I usually viewed these trips as sacrifices since they took me away from my family along with being tiring, if not exhausting. Once I made it to the airport, I usually appreciated the change in routine, and once I made it to the hotel, I usually appreciated the opportunities to meet new people, see new things, and discuss new ideas.

But I rarely took any extra time to explore the area on my own after the business was complete. Instead, I felt compelled to get back to my family and "be there" for them ASAP. (It occurs to me that this sounds downright crazy as I write it so many years later.) Thankfully, there was one time when a colleague and I decided to take an extra day to explore Rome on our own.

Thanks to this fun, flexible and very accommodating colleague, I had a great day as we explored the city. In fact, it was so enjoyable that I vowed to return "soon" with my husband and kids (14 and 9) so that they could explore these wonders too.

Thirteen months later, the four of us were sitting on a plane heading to Rome where we experienced, what later became known as, "the best vacation".

Work experiences often make us better parents. And sometimes we need to indulge ourselves in order to understand how to leverage those experiences so that they benefit the whole family.

About the author
Kathy Haselmaier is a mother, wife, and the editor of Working Parent Stories. She and her husband worked full-time while raising their children.

56
Post Business Trip Reunions

"FaceTime is amazing."
-- Savannah Guthrie --

When our kids were little I worried when I had to take long business trips because I feared that it wasn't good for them to have me gone for more than a few days. Now that they're grown, I know that those fears were silly, and I can see that there were many ways that those trips actually made me a better parent. The experiences were good for my kids.

Those thoughts re-surfaced as I watched a short video from NBC's TODAY show recently. It highlighted the anchors' two-week separations from their families, especially kids, while they were in South Korea covering the 2018 Winter Olympics, and it showed their homecomings too.

Working parents whose jobs require them to travel will probably be able to relate to the stories they tell. (And older working parents will be able to relate to the differences between returning to babies and toddlers vs. teenagers :) Google the video to see for yourself.

About the author
Kathy Haselmaier is a mother, wife, and the editor of *Working Parent Stories*. She and her husband worked full-time while raising their children.

HOLIDAY STORIES

4 stories

It's OK to make changes that result in more peace for you and those you love.

You don't need to do what everyone else is doing.

Create your own traditions.

57

The Pinnacle of Halloween Fun

by Mark Haselmaier

During Halloween my parents and I were on the same wavelength; this kid needs a costume, and it needs to rock

As a kid, Halloween was obviously a big deal. A costume ritual was involved. I would wear it around the house a couple of times before the big day (to make sure it worked and all), and then be near euphoria when it was finally time to reveal its awesomeness to the world.

I always considered myself lucky at Halloween because my parents took me to the store and let me pick out my own costume. Very rarely did we do stuff like that. Usually, if I wanted something, I either had to work around the house to earn enough money to pay for it, or I had to save money from my allowance to purchase what I wanted. But it felt like during Halloween my parents and I were on the same wavelength; this kid needs a costume, and it needs to rock.

So it came as a shock when just this past weekend my mother expressed embarrassment because she had to buy costumes all those years instead of making something more special. What? You're embarrassed? Why are you embarrassed about something that totally kicked ass? You let me pick out whatever I wanted from the costume aisle. That was the only time you let me just walk into a store and pick whatever I wanted and then you paid for it. For a Haselmaier child, this was almost unheard of.

After further discussion I learned that the purchase of a Halloween costume, instead of the creation of one, saved a lot of time for my working parents. It seems funny to me that they were embarrassed that they resorted to a store-bought costume at Halloween. For four-year-old me (and 11-year-old-me for that matter) it was the pinnacle of Halloween fun.

Chill out parents. You may be taking things a little too seriously.

About the author

Mark Haselmaier is a partner solutions coordinator for Oracle Data Cloud and the son of working parents. He earned a BS degree in Business Marketing from the University of Colorado at Boulder.

58
Holiday Perspective

What they *didn't* list was very interesting

When I think of the holidays, stress is the strongest feeling that washes over me. It shouldn't. At least not now. My kids are grown, and I have very little to worry about. But years and years of the real deal (i.e. stress) are hard to shake.

On Thanksgiving, I asked my kids (now 27 and 22) to list their top fun Christmas memories. Here's what they told me:

- Receiving a ping pong table
- The "emergency" trip to the airport ostensibly to "help some friends", when they were surprised to find Grandma and Grandpa getting off the plane instead of the expected friends' relatives
- Seeing a fox on the front porch on Christmas morning
- Receiving an iPod

- A Christmas morning scavenger hunt
- Artichokes for Christmas dinner
- Relaxing for multiple days

What they didn't list was even more interesting. They didn't mention the cooking, the cleaning, the decorating, or any of the million other little things that stressed me out each year. They didn't mention any of the holiday concerts or programs we dutifully attended. They didn't mention the way the ornaments were so neatly arranged on the tree. They didn't mention the vast selection of cookies we made, or any of the food prep really … well, except the artichokes we had that one year.

The scavenger hunt took place the year we were worried about money and gave them very little. It took them all morning and part of the afternoon to find very few gifts thanks to the never-ending trail of clues and the secret code that had to be deciphered.

These reflections have me thinking. Was my stress self-imposed? Was I trying to please my kids? Was I trying to please someone else? There is no doubt in my mind that a significant amount of my stress resulted from my desire to meet at least perceived expectations of others. And that leads me to wonder; what could each of us do to let others and ourselves off the hook this year?

Maybe one of the most valuable gifts we could give each other is the gift of lower expectations.

About the author
Kathy Haselmaier is a mother, wife, and the editor of Working Parent Stories. She and her husband worked full-time while raising their children.

59
What if … ?

Re-thinking some holiday activities

What if you didn't attend one of your child's holiday programs this year? Not all of them, just one. What if you explained to your child that sometimes, most of the time, he or she is your highest priority and that means that you miss other important things so that you can be with him or her? And what if you went on to explain that sometimes, when you know he or she is safe and happy, other things are a higher priority? Like people in need, planning for the future, or even your job?

Is it possible that action would give your child gifts that could last a lifetime? Might you give them the gift of learning to perform for others, not just you? Might you give him or her the gift of independence (if only for a few minutes)? Might you give him or her a gift they'll greatly appreciate in the future when, as a working parent, he or she knows for sure that a child can feel happy and loved without constant attention from parents?

Working parents throughout social media express frustrations during the holidays every year. They're frustrated when school holiday performances and activities are scheduled in the middle of the workday; they wonder how they're expected to be in two places at the same time. They want to be great parents and they want to be great employees. They become frustrated when the system appears to conspire against them.

It might make sense to ask your kids if they think it's important that you attend every single holiday activity. You might be surprised (and relieved) to hear their answers.

About the author
Kathy Haselmaier is a mother, wife, and the editor of Working Parent Stories. She and her husband worked full-time while raising their children.

60
Christmas Eve All-Nighter

by Kelly Irwin

Finishing an 18-hour shift on Christmas Eve day

Editor's Note: Lots of working parents make sacrifices so that the rest of us can enjoy the holidays. Here's a story from one of them. Thank you, Kelly!

On Christmas day I can't help but remember back to so many previous years when I slept most of the day. I worked for a grocery store chain in the deli department. We'd work all night making party trays that were ready for pick-up on Christmas Eve. I'd finish an 18-hour shift on Christmas Eve day.

One year was extra special. After working all night, I arrived at my friend George's house, and he asked me to be his wife. (I said yes :)

We worked hard so that people could have great holiday gatherings. I always fell asleep right after dinner on Christmas Eve and then slept well into Christmas day, almost missing the day completely.

My son recently commented, "You worked hard and dedicated your skills to make other people's holidays, Mom. You should feel proud knowing that you made great party trays for people. And from what I remember as a kid, you enjoyed it. Kudos to you."

He was right. I did love it. I'm very proud and blessed to have been able to do that kind of work. For the most part every job I've ever had has given me joy in one way or other.

About the author
Kelly Irwin is a mother and wife who spent 26 years working at Farmer Jack grocery stores, mostly in deli departments. She now provides help and personal care for senior citizens.

ABOUT WORKING PARENT STORIES

5 stories

·

Parents who are raising kids and working know that it isn't always easy.

That's why we admire them.

61

Why Focus on Working Parents?

Recently a hard-working and much-admired mother read one of our stories and commented that stay-at-home parents and working parents all want similar things. I totally agree. I've yet to meet a parent who isn't striving to do their best whether they work full-time, focus on their family full-time, or something in between. All parents I encounter seem to want the best for their children, their partner, their parents, their siblings, their friends, and their employer (when they have one). I'm guessing that there are people out there who aren't trying their hardest, but I don't know them. For years I've suggested that any parent who wants to make a case for leaving the workforce to stay home full-time should gather data points from working parents. We've got some real horror stories about our own missteps and the consequences, but we're careful about sharing them.

So why focus exclusively on stories of inspiration and encouragement for working parents?

1. **Volunteer work** focused on attracting and retaining women in STEM-related careers showed me first-hand the high value of role models and encouragement. Working Parent Stories showcase role models and offer encouragement.

2. **There are significantly more online resources** for stay-at-home parents than working parents. Stay-at-home parents are blogging and Tweeting at a staggering rate. Working parent support, encouragement, tips, and humor are harder to find. I have the network and know-how to provide some.

3. **Lack of experience as a stay-at-home parent** prevents me from adding any credible suggestions for them.

4. **The feedback has been very encouraging**. Working parents tell us they love the stories. It's hard to walk away from that ;)

The great thing about the Internet is that there is something for almost everyone. Stay-at-home moms are able to access a ton of info to support, encourage, and enhance their lifestyle. Stay-at-home dads are also popping up all over the blogosphere and on Twitter and Instagram. Some are especially funny and entertaining. And now, Working Parents have another resource designed to inspire, encourage, and support their lifestyle. Oh, and we try to find a little humor in our missteps too. Thank you for reading the stories!

About the author
Kathy Haselmaier is a mother, wife, and the editor of *Working Parent Stories*. She and her husband worked full-time while raising their children. Kathy worked in high tech marketing and business operations roles after earning a BS degree in Computer Science from Michigan Tech.

62
Beyond the Benefits

How employers can improve employee retention among working parents

As the editor of *Working Parent Stories*, you probably won't be surprised to read that I've gotten to know a lot of working parents ... and their stories. A common theme has emerged that is rarely discussed. We're used to hearing about the need for better benefits and more flexibility within the workplace as a way of enticing more women to remain in the workforce, and most agree that these things are valued by all working parents and probably most employees. But something mentioned less often, and a theme that is emerging in many working parent stories, is that subtle messages are being sent to working mothers that can affect their determination to purse their careers and maintain the energy needed to succeed. The messages are sent by friends, relatives, and the media. They question a woman's commitment to her family when she chooses to pursue a career. I call these messages "micro discouragements".

Every woman knows that if she has a child she will need to make "the choice"; will she return to work or exit the workforce after the baby arrives? Sometimes the choice is made with a partner. And sometimes there is no choice because returning to work is a necessity. Most men aren't yet expected to make "the choice". But as more and more women out-earn their partners, more and more men are finding they need to make "the choice" too.

Recently I heard someone comment that working mothers often manage their careers like their fathers (who often had full-time "assistants" at home) while trying to mother like their stay-at-home moms. And some working fathers have few, if any, role models from dual-career couples. Some people dismiss these generalizations as outdated, but stories from young working parents suggest that the struggle is still very real for many of them. Even today.

If you're a man balancing fatherhood with a demanding career that requires hard work every day, every week, and every month, imagine the joy of a holiday gathering with family (which, of course, involves more and different work at home). And then imagine the feeling you'll experience when your father quietly asks you, "How's work going? How sure are you that pursuing your career is really best? Isn't Kelsey's career going well enough to enable you to be at home with the kids?" Could it feel a little like a punch in the gut? A "micro discouragement"? Could a steady stream of these messages start to undermine your enthusiasm, resolve, and energy?

Many women who have careers are enduring these micro discouragements on a regular basis. Even today. They come from well-meaning parents, friends, aunts and uncles, the Internet, other parents, TV, cousins, magazines, people at church, and the radio. More and more men may start to endure them too. Some women let them roll off their backs and never give them a second thought. Some women are energized by them because they represent a challenge.

But some women don't find these comments energizing at all. These are the women who are at risk of dropping out of the workforce or have already. These are the women who struggle to maintain the energy needed to juggle multiple roles that include a career. These are the women who are often at risk of leaving your company or maybe the workforce entirely. These are the women who can't fully enjoy the satisfaction of a job well done within the context of a career.

So what can employers do? First, it's probably worth noting that you can't afford to provide enough benefits to impress "Aunt Susie" or "Tiffany" at the PTA meeting. No matter how much flexibility and assistance you offer your working parents, some of their friends and relatives are likely to continue delivering "micro discouragements", at least for the foreseeable future. So employers need to find ways to neutralize and overcome the effects of the "micro discouragements" with "micro encouragements". They need to help working parents more clearly recognize the benefits their work provides to their families. The data is out there, and employers need to find ways to get it in front of their employees. They can also pair young working parents with older working parents who've mastered the balance. They can share stories of success within their own companies via web sites, videos, and newsletters. They can create forums so that working parents can encourage each other, discuss challenges, and share best practices.

Find ways to provide "micro encouragements" to young working parents, and then reap the rewards for years to come.

About the author
Kathy Haselmaier is a mother, wife, and the editor of *Working Parent Stories*. She and her husband worked full-time while raising their children. Kathy worked in high tech marketing and business

operations roles after earning a BS degree in Computer Science from Michigan Technological University.

63
Top 8 Surprises

From the first 50 stories published on the web site

These stories contained a few predictable themes, but collectively they produced the following surprises:

1. Many men confidently, quickly and clearly articulate how their work inspires them to parent. Of the first 50 stories, 22 were from men. None of them mentioned a concern that working might diminish their role as a father.

2. Many women mentioned that they enjoy their work. Interestingly men didn't mention this often or maybe ever. I'm guessing that a lot of men do enjoy their work, but they didn't mention that in their stories.

3. Some new fathers find it difficult to return to work after their babies are born.

4. Meal prep is a challenge for many dual career couples, and there are a lot of men doing a lot of food prep in those families. This topic resulted in a lot of comments!

5. Not one story submitter has complained that their employer hinders their ability to be a good parent. There is a lot of social media chatter about the need for more flexibility in the workplace and better childcare, but nobody mentioned those topics in these stories.

6. Many working parents believe that their need to focus on work has been a positive influence on their children. Sometimes this wasn't by design and the value was only realized in hindsight.

7. Executives with very demanding careers appear to be great parents too. This is probably because they apply the same strong skills that have propelled them in the workplace when they're raising their kids.

8. Working Parent limitations sometimes result in valuable lessons for their kids.

About the author
Kathy Haselmaier is a mother, wife, and the editor of *Working Parent Stories*. She and her husband worked full-time while raising their children.

64
Top 6 Learnings

From the second 50 stories published on the web site

These stories produced the following learnings:

1. Working parents are trying very hard to be great parents and great employees. Parents repeatedly described the significant efforts they put forth to be the best parents possible while delivering strong contributions at work.

2. Some working fathers are starting to face "the choice". As more women are out-earning their spouses, men are sometimes forced to chose between careers and managing the home full-time.

3. Working mothers are often clear about the fact that they want to set a good example for their kids. Mothers often talk about their strong desires to set good examples for their children via their careers.

4. Some working parents manage "special needs" in addition to traditional parenting and careers. These parents are juggling even more than many others. They're inspiring!

5. Some working mothers still endure a steady stream of "micro discouragements". Even though most parents work outside the home, some mothers still find their commitment to their families questioned (often subtly) when they pursue careers.

6. Working parents in 29 countries are reading these stories.

About the author
Kathy Haselmaier is a mother, wife, and the editor of *Working Parent Stories*. She and her husband worked full-time while raising their children.

65
Top 11 Insights

From the third 50 stories published on the web site

These stories produced the following 11 insights:

1. Current thinking is that a fulfilling career is an important component of a complete life.
2. Most Working Parents possess more power than they realize to achieve their career goals.
3. Many kids are proud of their parents' careers.
4. A working spouse who encourages your career can provide a great career advantage.
5. New mothers are pushing new boundaries in terms of pursuing career opportunities.
6. Role models make a difference.
7. Skills learned on the job often make us better parents.

8. Kids who are watched too closely can be handicapped in the moment and as adults. Because working parents juggle many roles, they are theoretically less likely to handicap their children in this way.

9. Working parents are willing to publicly express the strong emotions associated with parenthood without feeling like it undermines their career opportunities.

10. Working parents continue to juggle many roles.

11. *Working Parent Stories* readers span 54 countries.

About the author
Kathy Haselmaier is a mother, wife, and the editor of *Working Parent Stories*. She and her husband worked full-time while raising their children.

THOUGHT-PROVOKING

7 stories

*If you really want to do something,
you'll find a way.
If you don't, you'll find an excuse.*

-- Jim Rohn --

66

Employer, Spouse or You?

What's the real reason parents walk away from their careers?

Yesterday I heard a parent on the radio explain that she left her career because her employer wouldn't give her the flexibility she needed as a parent. Given that I had the radio on for about 90 seconds, I didn't hear what she said before she made that comment, and I heard very little after it, but I was left wondering; did her spouse also need to leave his career? And if not, why not? Is it possible that her spouse wasn't helping to provide the flexibility she needed to continue her career? Or maybe she didn't want to truly share parental responsibilities with him. Did she ask him for more help?

Sometimes it seems like people are looking for reasons to avoid pursuing a career instead of ways to make it work.

About the author
Kathy Haselmaier is a mother, wife, and the editor of *Working Parent Stories*. She and her husband worked full-time while raising their children. Kathy worked in high tech marketing and business operations roles after earning a BS degree in Computer Science from Michigan Tech.

67
Don't Do What I Did

by Thomas McFall
adapted from Twitter with permission | @Thomas___McFall

Some working parents make unusually significant sacrifices

In one of my Management classes, I sit in the same seat every day. It's in the front of the class. Every single day I sit there.

It's next to some foreign guy who barely speaks English. The most advanced thing I've heard this guy say in English is "Wow, my muffin is really good". This guy also has a habit of stacking every item he owns in the exact space I sit; his bag, his food, his books, and his phone are ALWAYS right on my desk space.

Every single time I walk into class this guy says "Ah, Tom. You here. Okay." And then he starts frantically clearing my desk of his belongings. He then makes it a habit to say "Ready for class, yeah?"

And gives me a high five. Every day this guy gives me a high five.

I was ALWAYS annoyed with this guy. I'm thinking "Dude, you know I sit in this seat every day. Why are you always stacking your shit here? And the last thing I want to do is give a guy who barely speaks my language high fives at 8:00 in the morning." Just get your shit off my desk.

But Monday I came to class and was running a few minutes late. I'm standing outside because I had to send a quick text. Out of the corner of my eye, I could see my usual space through the door. Of course, my desk was filled with his belongings. The usual.

As I'm standing there on my phone, another guy, who was also late, walks into the class before me and tried to take my seat since it's closest to the door. The foreign guy who sits next to me stops this dude from sitting down and says "I'm sorry. My good friend Thomas sits here."

It was then that I realized this guy wasn't putting stuff on my seat to annoy me. He was saving me the seat every morning. And this whole time he saw me as a friend, but I was too busy thinking about myself to take him into consideration. Cheesy as it sounds, I was touched.

I ended up going into class, and of course he cleared the seat and said "Ah, Tom. You here. Okay." And I did get a high five. At the end of class I asked him if he wanted to get a bite to eat with me. We did. And we talked for a while. I got through the broken English and learned that he moved here from the Middle East to pursue a college education in America. He plans to go back after he gets his degree. He's got two kids and a wife. He works full time and sends all his leftover money back home to his wife.

Moral of the story? Don't do what I did and constantly only think about yourself. It took me nearly the entire semester to get my head out of my ass and realize this guy was just trying to be my friend. Better late than never I suppose.

About the author
Thomas McFall is a business major at Youngstown State University in Ohio. His new friend is a parent, husband, and student who also works full time. Follow Thomas via Twitter @Thomas___McFall.

68
La Charge Mentale

A French term for the mental load associated with managing a household that usually falls to the woman

This is a topic I had been avoiding, but when a working mother from Europe contacted me directly, asked me to address it, and provided some research results, well ... I felt compelled to share my perspective.

Who is the Chief Operating Officer (COO) of your household? By this I mean, who makes sure that the children are fed, clothed, and clean? Who makes sure birthday parties are planned, gifts are purchased, and thank you notes are sent? Who makes sure your house guests have clean sheets, holiday gatherings occur (every year), and summer vacations (and other travel) get planned? Who makes sure that all of the details of your lives are managed so that you and your children are included in social circles, teachers and friends don't worry about your family, and your household functions like a well-oiled machine ... or at least a machine that runs?

According to lots of research (in both the US and Europe), mothers are most often the COO of the family. Does this mean that dads aren't carrying their weight and providing strong contributions within a family? Well, it sounds like that depends on the family. But apparently, within a lot of families, women don't feel like the load is being shared fairly, and there is research to support those feelings.

As I mentioned, I had been avoiding this topic; I haven't been reading the articles. But, I do understand the frustration, I have experienced the frustration, and I do believe that I have eliminated the frustration. So I will share my story.

For as long as I can remember, I've had a strategic vision for parenting. I knew how I wanted to raise my kids, I knew what I wanted to teach my kids, and I knew what kind of an environment I wanted to create for my family. Right down to whether or not feet would be allowed on the coffee table. And then I had kids. It turns out that I needed to adjust a bit, because, guess what? My kids are not just like me. (That was a big shock.) So I adjusted.

If my husband had a strategic vision for raising our kids, he hasn't shared it with me yet. Maybe that's an overstatement, but I think it's accurate to say that he was a lot more open minded and flexible than I was. But ... he did seem to have a strategic vision for his career. I can't say I ever had that. I wasn't totally sure that I'd even have a career until well after our daughter was born. My career always felt like more of an experiment (with big ramifications for the family).

My husband and I worked at the same company, so we were able to observe each other at work and at home. Not all that long ago, I realized that my husband was very strategic at work, but very tactical at home. I, on the other hand, was very strategic at home, and much more tactical at work. The thing is, there was no way we were going to manage two demanding careers and two equally demanding kids unless we were both "all in" at work and at home.

Early in our marriage, I read multiple articles that pointed out that men weren't real enthused about taking on household tasks and chores when their wives recognized those efforts with criticism, suggestions for improvement, and sometimes even hostility. So I set out to encourage my husband to be a full-partner at home by accepting and encouraging his participation, even when I thought he did a sloppy job. And guess what? I couldn't do it. At least not all of the time. (I do believe this is a personality flaw which I totally own.) But I also couldn't do everything myself, so I was determined to find a way to make things work. We tried hard, together, to figure out what I could give up and what I couldn't, who was better at any given task, and who could manage which tasks most efficiently.

This means that he does all of the cooking, grocery shopping, and car maintenance. He mows the lawn, fixes the computers, and manages our investments. He was the one who got up with the kids in the middle of the night, he keeps in touch with everyone in his family, and he is best at texting our (now grown) kids regularly. And every once in a while he takes on something I didn't want to give up, but have to out of sheer desperation. Sometimes he does those things in a way that is super successful (and beyond what I've even thought to request).

If you want to be a good spouse, avoid resenting your spouse, teach your kids how to be great spouses, and keep yourself healthy, I think you need to figure out how to resolve this issue. And by "resolve it", I mean you're probably going to need to discuss this topic with your spouse a lot in the early years of your marriage, regularly in the middle of your marriage, and sometimes late in your marriage. When people say that marriage is hard, this is one of the things they're talking about. The fact that you and your spouse are willing to tackle this issue, over and over and over, means that you are committed to your partnership. It's one of the biggies.

So you may be wondering what I do while my husband makes dinner. This is a question I get a lot. If you're a working mom, you know the answer. If you don't know the answer, ask your spouse.

About the author
Kathy Haselmaier is a mother, wife, and the editor of *Working Parent Stories*. She and her husband worked full-time while raising their children. Kathy worked in high tech marketing and business operations roles after earning a BS degree in Computer Science from Michigan Tech.

69
Risks and Rewards

"There is real harm in keeping an eye on the kids if you're keeping an eye on them every minute of every day."
-- Ashley Thomas --

When our kids were growing up they flew alone from Denver to Detroit every summer to visit their grandparents in the Mitten State. They took their first trips when they were seven and eight-years-old and were so intent on going alone, they insisted on being there different weeks. Maximizing a rare chance for some undivided attention was probably their primary motivator.

Most of our friends and co-workers knew about the ritual, and I distinctly remember the time one of my co-workers, my manager actually, told me, "I would never let my children travel alone on an airplane." Apparently she wasn't impressed with our attempt to foster a strong sense of independence in our kids while ensuring some quality time with Grandma and Grandpa. Instead, she thought we were putting them at great risk. And I assume she thought the risk was greater than any potential reward.

This memory was triggered recently when a friend pointed me to an article written by Tania Lombrozo that was published on the NPR web site in 2016. It's called "Why Do We Judge Parents For Putting Kids at Perceived - But Unreal - Risk?" and references research* published in the open access journal *Collabra*. The article and research provide really fascinating, and sometimes surprising, information about how we perceive various parenting risks, and it draws attention to some thought-provoking ideas like the following:

- Driving a child to school generally puts them at greater risk of being harmed than letting them walk to school or ride a school bus.
- Leaving a child alone in a parked car generally decreases the child's risk of being killed when compared to walking them through a parking lot.

Working parents need to make a lot of deliberate decisions about childcare, and this article makes it clear that society judges those decisions ... sometimes harshly. And sometimes unfairly and ignorantly. This article will get you thinking, hard, about making decisions that will help your children both short-term and long-term. It may build your confidence in terms of decisions you've made or are making. Or it may cause you to question some decisions. Either way, it'll make you think.

File this story under "Fresh Thinking". And at least try to skim the article. It's really fascinating.

* More about the research: It included a series of clever experiments written by authors Ashley Thomas, Kyle Stanford and Barbara Sarnecka. They found evidence that shifting people's moral attitudes toward a parent influences the perceived risk to that parent's unattended child.

About the author
Kathy Haselmaier is a mother, wife, and the editor of *Working Parent Stories*. She and her husband worked full-time while raising their children. Kathy worked in high tech marketing and business operations roles after earning a BS degree in Computer Science from Michigan Tech.

70

Choices and Consequences

In a nutshell; choices have consequences

The gender pay gap gets a lot of attention. Many theories try to explain why it exists. While many spend time speculating and theorizing about it, the folks at Uber have gathered data that provides new insights. People who value fair pay, including working parents, are likely to find this info pretty interesting. (And those who want to dig deeper into the data can listen to the *Freakonomics* podcast "What Can Uber Teach Us About the Gender Pay Gap?")

Some believe that the gender pay gap could be reduced if workers had more flexible work hours. Uber offers its drivers total flexibility when it comes to hours worked.

Some assert that those who control pay have unconscious (or conscious) biases that result in men being paid more than women for the same work. Uber pays drivers using a gender-blind formula based on the length of a ride in miles and minutes. Additionally, the fare (which determines pay) may include "multipliers" based on customer demand at any given time. Uber's pay structure is based solely on services provided, and it's non-negotiable.

Some think that hiring can be a biased process, and we agree. At Uber work is assigned via an undeniably gender-blind process.

This means that Uber is able to provide driver pay data that is virtually devoid of gender biases. As you might imagine, researchers were eager to sift through this data. And, for a variety of reasons, they expected women Uber drivers to out-earn men by just a little or at the very least to earn the same amount as men on an hourly basis. But guess what? That's not happening.

The data shows that men make about 7% more per hour (on average) for doing the exact same job. And remember, this is in a setting where work assignments are made by a gender-blind algorithm, and the pay structure is tied directly to output and is non-negotiable. Interestingly, this 7% pay gap aligns with gender pay gaps uncovered by other studies within other work environments.

So how do they explain this?! Before jumping to the answer, it's worth noting that the volume of data available for analysis was huge; 25M driver-weeks across 196 US cities over 22 months (June 2015 - March 2017). It included >1.8M drivers and >740M Uber trips.

As the researchers dug deep into the data, here's what they found:

Men and women Uber drivers make different choices about when they drive and which routes they choose. These choices impact the value of the trips and therefore their pay. (e.g. Men drive more late-night hours which pay well and women drive more Sunday afternoons which pay well.) The choices they make account for ~20% of the gap. These choices hint at a deeper issue too.

Driver experience influences choices. Large returns can result when drivers apply the experience they gain on the job. Basically, the more you drive, the more you learn and the more you earn. Experience helps drivers get better at figuring out where and when to drive and then how to strategically accept or cancel rides to maximize income. Men and women appear to learn at the same rate, but men spend more time driving, so they are able to figure out how to maximize their income faster. This accounts for another ~30% of the gap.

Finally, men complete more trips per hour than women. This is because they drive slightly (~2%) faster. And Uber feedback indicates that riders value faster rides. This choice accounts for the final ~50% of the gap. (Interestingly, studies show that, on average, men also drive slightly faster than women even when they aren't Uber drivers, although women have more crashes. But men have more fatal crashes, so it isn't clear whether men or women tend to be the safer drivers on average.)

So while women have every opportunity to earn just as much as men when they're Uber drivers, the choices they make are lowering their average income slightly. In a nutshell, choices have consequences.

This info is compelling for working parents because it makes it really clear that career choices always have consequences. A decision to opt out of the workforce, for even a relatively short period of time like a year, can have lasting consequences. Usually we understand that and are happy to live with the consequences. But sometimes people don't understand that even a short "break" from the workforce in the early years of a career will result in unexpected and significant consequences (not to mention frustrations) down the road.

Working while raising kids is hard, but this data shows that those who figure how to make it work are more likely to find themselves satisfied over the long run if equal pay is important to them. We probably shouldn't be surprised to learn that Uber and the researchers have just confirmed that experience matters and hard work pays off.

About the research
Freakonomics has been called "the most readable economics blog in the universe". Learn more about this story via the Freakonomics podcast called "What Can Uber Teach Us About the Gender Pay Gap?"

About the commentator
Kathy Haselmaier is a mother, wife, and the editor of *Working Parent Stories*. She and her husband worked full-time while raising their children. Kathy worked in high tech marketing and business operations roles after earning a BS degree in Computer Science from Michigan Tech.

71

What Can I Do About It?

When it comes to the gender pay gap, you may have more power than you think

Most parents want their children to be paid fairly when they enter the workforce. They believe that compensation should correlate to value delivered, and that an employee's gender should not impact their pay. Many are passionate about the topic of "equal pay for equal work", and we write about some of them in the final story "When Parents Mange Income the Same Way Corporations Manage Revenue".

The first step toward achieving equal pay is working (i.e. obtaining some pay ;). Then, if you want to compare your compensation to another employee's pay, you need to produce at least the same results or value as that person. Some fascinating data about the gender pay gap was published in the Working Parent Story called "Choices and Consequences". Some studies show that pay rates for men and women align until the birth of their first child. After that, women who have a child find that, on average, their pay dips. Many factors explain the dip, and some people are bothered by it.

Researchers from Princeton, the London School of Economics, and the Danish Ministry of Taxation recently found that in Denmark, one of the greatest predictors for how a woman's pay will be impacted by having a child is the example set by her mother. Specifically, the example her mother sets in terms of how she manages her career. Apparently men's pay, on average, dips very little, if any, after their first child is born. You can read about this research in a short article in *The Economist* called "The roots of the gender pay gap lie in childhood" (Jan 26, 2018).

So, if you're serious about wanting your daughter to be compensated at the same rate as the men she will work with, look no further than the example set within your own family.

Related note: A guy I know recently commented that we often give mothers most of the credit, as well as the blame, related to their children's opportunities and behaviors. We agree. At the same time, many couples believe that childrearing is a team effort, and neither parent's contribution is more important than the other's. Congratulations to all of the parents working so hard to support their children, each other, and their communities. It isn't easy, and that's why we admire you!

About the author

Kathy Haselmaier is a mother, wife, and the editor of *Working Parent Stories*. She and her husband worked full-time while raising their children. Kathy worked in high tech marketing and business operations roles after earning a BS degree in Computer Science from Michigan Tech.

72

When Parents Manage Income the Same Way Corporations Manage Revenue

Why do people claim to want change as they perpetuate stereotypes and reinforce the norm?

Editor's Note: *The convenient thing about writing stories you edit is that you can have conversations, and even debates, with yourself. This story is categorized as "thought-provoking", so let's be clear up-front; I am not suggesting that full-time work is something that every parent will want to pursue, nor should they. Mindful parents make choices that support their unique visions for their families. The purpose of this piece is to stretch minds and encourage people to think and talk about how we can improve things for everyone.*

A casually asserted online comment got me thinking recently. It stated that an earnings gap between women and men is the reason many young women opt out of the workforce after they have children. It wasn't the first time I'd read the claim, and I doubt it will be the last.

The comment left me wondering; why do many affluent parents prioritize disposable income over things they claim to value more? Things like equal pay for equal work, fair opportunities for advancement in the workplace, and shared responsibilities at home. How do we explain this behavior? (i.e. How do we interpret parents' decisions about career priorities which are based on current income generated and/or incomes imagined in the future?) When corporations prioritize revenue and profit over other things, some label them as "greedy". When parents prioritize disposable income over things they claim to value more, do some assume they're motivated by greed too?

It appears that disposable income is a very high priority when affluent women say they drop out of the workforce because they don't earn as much money as their husbands.

Many young parents find ways to manage both career and family responsibilities, but young women are still leaving the workforce at greater rates than young men. (A 2012 McKinsey Study calls this the "leaky pipeline".) These exits perpetuate stereotypes that suggest women aren't as committed to careers as men. They also send messages to employers who find themselves in a bit of a bind; they value the strong contributions from women, but can't ignore the risks associated with employing them. Since women drop out of the workforce at greater rates than men, the following logical consequences often occur:

Organizations (i.e. the people who work within them) continue to make decisions based on the assumption that training and engaging young women provides lower average ROIs (Returns on Investment) than similar investments in men (because women are more likely to opt-out of the workforce).

The women who remain in the workplace need to invest incremental energy as they strive to assure their employers they're committed to their careers and therefore deserve the same compensation and advancement opportunities as their male peers.

Stereotypes are reinforced. Employers notice (and children do too).

Women who opt out of the workforce aren't the only ones that increase the burden for the women who stay. Women who settle for jobs that don't demand their full potential reinforce the stereotype that women aren't capable of handling as much responsibility or pressure as men. This can negatively influence the kinds of opportunities that are available to the women who are striving to reach their full potential.

But the fact that young women opt out of the workforce at greater rates than young men, or don't always pursue career challenges as vigorously as men, doesn't always hurt women in the workplace. Most organizations value the benefits provided by diverse work teams and some women possess unique skills or perform at exceptional levels, so in some cases, and especially in male-dominated organizations, the women who remain find themselves receiving special attention and unique benefits. One young mother recently told me, "My husband and I work at the same level and for the same FANG company (i.e. Facebook, Amazon, Netflix, Google). We are expecting our first baby soon. Our benefits will provide me with three months of paid medical leave after the baby is born, and then we are both able to take three months of paid parental leave too. It's pretty much assumed that I will take the entire leave. It's also assumed that I am a flight risk, may not return, or I am likely to want part time or flex time if I return. My husband, on the other hand, is not considered a flight risk, and it is assumed he won't want to change his current situation at all. Interestingly I actually end up with way more options. The company is willing to bend over backward to keep me and has proactively offered me part time or extended personal leave options even though I haven't even hinted that I'm interested in any of these things. It's not the same for my husband. He thinks that requesting these options might be career limiting or refused entirely." (If you're looking for a reason to encourage your young daughter to consider non-traditional career options, you may have found it in this comment.)

People who are truly committed to influencing change must be willing to make at least some small sacrifices. To influence positive change we need to stand on principle to do the "right" thing instead of the easy, comfortable, or "greedy" thing. Complaining our way to change rarely works. We need to do the hard work of making it happen. We need to take action and lead by example.

Women can make things better by participating in the workforce, striving to contribute at higher levels, and showing the world what is possible. Men can support the cause by being consistent cheerleaders and encouraging women to participate in the workforce at levels that utilizes their full potential (not only in roles that are traditional and/or comfortable). Women and men need to be willing to share more responsibilities. For women this may mean striving to achieve more professionally; for men this may mean taking on more food prep, clean up and carpool tasks. People who are managers and in other positions of influence need to advocate for working parents and fair policies. We all need to let go of outdated expectations and do more of the "right" things.

We have the power to create the change we want. Let's use it. Nobody has more to gain from this kind of progress than our own children.

About the author
Kathy Haselmaier is a mother, wife, and the editor of *Working Parent Stories*. She and her husband worked full-time while raising their children. Kathy worked in high tech marketing and business operations roles after earning a BS degree in Computer Science from Michigan Technological University.

More Working Parent Stories

More stories (and videos) are posted at
www.WorkingParentStories.com
New stories are added regularly.

Follow Working Parent Stories via:
Twitter @Working_Parents
Instagram @Working_Parent_Stories
Facebook: Working Parent Stories
LinkedIn: Working Parent Stories
Pinterest: Working Parent Stories
Reddit: WorkingParentStories
Email Newsletter:
www.WorkingParentStories.com/subscribe

Every working parent has stories.
We want to hear yours.
Submit stories here:
www.WorkingParentStories.com/submit

www.ingramcontent.com/pod-product-compliance
Lightning Source LLC
LaVergne TN
LVHW051113080426
835510LV00018B/2011